VICTORIA DE LOS ANGELES

VICTORIA DE LOS ANGELES

Peter Roberts

Weidenfeld & Nicolson
LONDON

Designed and produced by Breslich & Foss
43 Museum Street, London WC1A 1LY

Copyright © 1982 Peter Roberts

Published in Great Britain by
Weidenfeld and Nicolson Limited
91 Clapham High Street
London SW4 7TA

ISBN 0 297 78099 9

Text set in 11/14pt Linotron 202 Century, printed and bound
in Great Britain at The Pitman Press, Bath

Contents

FOR R.L.R.

To list all the generous people I have been allowed to consult in the course of preparing this book would in itself make a chapter. So I must be content with thanking Victoria de los Angeles herself for her patient collaboration over the years, for revisiting with me scenes of her childhood in Spain and for allowing me to ply her with questions not only in her home in Barcelona but wherever else they materialised—in dressing-rooms, in restaurants, in taxis, in airport lobbies. Her patience and good humour have been inexhaustible. For the loan of valuable reference material I thank Antonio Fernandez Cid, José Maria Lamaña, Salvador Moreno and members of the de los Angeles family in Spain and, in England, Frank Granville Barker, Peter Bettany, David Bicknell and Michael Letchford. In London the treasure troves of the archives of *Opera* magazine and *The Gramophone* have been indispensable.

P.R.

1

Catalonia is a nation within Spain. Ever since the Romans colonised her and established the port of Barcelona as her capital, Catalonia has been an independent melting-pot of cultural and genetic influences. Venetian, Phoenician, Italian and French traders and mariners brought news of artistic and scientific developments to Barcelona. They also brought their temperaments, their blood, and each race has stamped the Catalan just as each has stamped the city.

The Catalan has his own language, which he cherishes in the face of economic and social pressure. Catalonia has learned to absorb and to integrate disparate influences. From many peoples, there has sprung one, with a fiercely proud national identity. The Catalan is hard-working, stubborn and resolutely independent, as Franco was to find, to his cost. The arts are an essential, integral part of his daily life. Poets Lope de Vega, Jiménez, Galdos, Lorca and Alarcón were reared in Catalonia. Dali comes from Figueras, a town near Barcelona. Picasso, Miró and Gris all moved to Paris from Barcelona. The harlequins, acrobats and beggars of Picasso's 'blue' period are all to be seen in the poor quarters of the city today.

But if there is one characteristic of Barcelona which all visitors remember, one trait which is common to all Catalans, it is the love of music. Barcelona boasts one of the world's largest opera houses and concert halls. On Sunday nights, and throughout September, the streets are full of the sound of the *Sardana*. To the oboe, the cymbals, the tambourine and the coplas, the Catalans dance in a circle, hand in hand through the night.

Spaniards do not put their children to bed early. When parents go down to the *Plaza del Teatro* for an evening's drinking and dancing, the children come too. They clutch their parents' hands, their eyes half-closed. And all around them, from the cafés and the taverns, come the smell of fish and *tapas*, the constant burble of conversation, and the sound of the *Sardana*. It was the first music to catch the souls of Albéniz and of Granados, of Pablo Casals, another distinguished native, and of a little girl who often walked the narrow streets down by the harbour with her parents: a poor girl named Victoria de los Angeles López García.

The story of Victoria's life is the story of a Catalan, whose career in music was to make her feel that she belonged to the whole of Spain and not just to her birthplace of Catalonia. Once again, Barcelona demonstrates its ability to absorb and to adopt alien influences. Bernardo López, Victoria's father, was born in Fuengirola, then a mere fishing village, now an Andalusian tourist trap full of jerry-built hotels and expensive *urbanisaciones*. Victoria García, her mother, came from a little Castilian village called Pueblo de Sanabria. The only connection between the two, born hundreds of miles apart, was that both had relatives working at Barcelona University. When they found too few opportunities in their native towns and sought their fortunes in a city, both headed for Barcelona.

They met, they married, and at first lived with Bernardo's mother. Bernardo had by this time acquired a job as one of the university porters, and his wife was a cleaner on the staff. Victoria was born in the hospital clinic attached to the medical faculty on November 1, All Saint's Day, 1923. Bernardo was 32, her mother 31. They had been married for four years, and already had one daughter, Carmen, who was three years older than Victoria.

2

'Poor Father, he was desperate for a son,' Victoria remembers. 'One day, when I was old enough to consider it, but still too young to understand, I asked him why.

"Because of the name," he said.

"Because of what name?"

"Our name, López, of course. I want a boy to carry on our name."

"But Father, *everyone* is called López."

'I don't think it amused him much', Victoria smiles. 'But three years later, he was granted his wish. His third and last child was a boy. He was christened José, but, as with all Josés, everyone has always called him Pepe.'

Everyone has to be appeased at a Spanish christening. 'The *de los Angeles* comes from my mother's brother Angel, who was also my godfather. Then, of course, we had to have Victoria for my mother's family, so I ended up as Victoria de los Angeles López García.

'There were problems about the name, actually. You see, Maria de los Angeles was a common name, and quite acceptable to the powers that be, but I was the first Victoria de los Angeles. We had to get special permission from the priest to use that combination.'

For several years before Victoria was born, the family lived a hand-to-mouth existence in Bernardo's mother's house. Then Bernardo was promoted to caretaker, and they moved into an apartment of their own in one of the university's twin turrets. It was to become their home, and Victoria was not to leave it until she, like her brother and her sister, married and made her own home.

The quarter of a century from the November when Victoria was born in 1923 until the November she was married in 1948 could hardly have been more difficult for a working class family with no inherited wealth to offset the hardships of a very troubled 25 years for Spain. In fact, in the year in which Victoria was born the country had run into such difficulties that King Alfonso XIII appointed the dictator Primo de Rivera to rule the country. But, by 1931, Rivera himself had been discredited and Alfonso had abdicated. Well-intentioned

3

but weak Republican governments followed, only to collapse in the Civil War declared on July 18, 1936. They were not easy years to bring up a family—least of all in Barcelona, where the people were bombed into the submission which ended Spain's war in March 1939. All vestiges of freedom and autonomy were to disappear during General Franco's long reign.

'I think we pulled through because my parents complemented each other so well. It is extraordinary how disaster makes people pull together and, above all, how resolutely cheerful everyone seems to be in the face of hardship. No one exemplified this better than my mother. Things must have been very, very tough for her, but in front of us she was always laughing. Students, too, could always count on a welcome in our apartment over the Chemistry faculty. There was an enormous terracotta coloured coffee-pot constantly on the hob and the front door was always open. It soon became an accepted feature of the students' social life to wander up between lectures for a cup of coffee and a chat.

'My mother was never still for a moment. There was always something to do. Even when the day's work was done she had to keep busy. She loved crochet and embroidery, and as the years went by, all the furniture and curtains in the apartment were covered with her embroidery.'

Victoria's mother seems to have appreciated living high above the earth. Remembering the narrow dark streets of her native Castille, she told her children how lucky they were to have so much light and air. When the going was particularly tough, she could still draw consolation from this small blessing. At least they did not have to live and work at street or basement level in the dingy poor quarters of the city.

But one day Victoria was playing hide-and-seek. She had taken refuge behind an old sofa, lovingly and laboriously restored by her mother's needlework. Suddenly she heard her mother sobbing, her father's voice gentle and soothing. Victoria did not dare to make her presence known, but shrank down further. Incredulous, she heard that there was no money for the evening meal. Some second-hand clothes were

4

going cheap, clothes which the children desperately needed. If only she had just a little money. . . . Bernardo comforted his wife and promised that somehow, somewhere, he would find enough money to tide them over. Only then did Victoria realise that the contentment of the family depended upon constant worry, overwork and deprivation.

While Victoria's mother was hardly ever ill, her father had been subject to chronic asthma ever since he joined the university staff as an assistant gardener at the age of fifteen. But no matter how much he wheezed he refused to think of himself as sick. A little over five feet tall, he was a restless, bustling, tireless man. 'He, too, was totally incapable of sitting back and doing nothing.'

No matter how industrious Bernardo might be, his earnings as a caretaker were too low to keep his family fed and clothed. Spain, at best never rich, was soon to be crippled by its long civil struggle. International trade was hampered by the roller-coaster markets of the 'twenties and 'thirties and by the growing tensions which were to explode into war. And Barcelona, blasted by bombs and financially dependent upon its trading port, felt these influences more keenly than any other Spanish town. There simply was not enough money to go round. Every weekday morning, therefore, saw the López parents up and working by five o'clock. Victoria's mother set off in the dawn twilight with buckets and brushes to scrub the steps and patios of the university. Bernardo's first job of the day, and the one which found most favour with the children, was making early morning deliveries of bread, *churros* and other pastries for a cake shop.

'It was a great treat', Victoria remembers, 'to wake up as he crept in after his rounds with a hot pastry for each of us children.'

In the evenings, the tireless Bernardo put another skill to use. As a boy in the Andalusian fishing village where he was born, he had learned to make nets and hammocks—a valuable craft in a large fishing port like Barcelona. Bernardo's resourcefulness obtained for him a variety of jobs which, although doubtless tawdry and tiresome, afforded him an

5

aura of glamour in his children's eyes. They were very impressed that, as a young man, he had been so small that he had been chosen to be lowered on ropes to lay the charges for tunnelling south of Barcelona. He had even been paid danger money. As a married man with four dependants he no longer took such risks, but his jobs seemed no less exciting. In the evenings he used to go down to a large open bar in the old town and work as a primitive sort of disc jockey. He operated an ancient pianola. The customers made requests, Bernardo collected their money and put on the selected numbers.

There were, too, plenty of jobs within the university itself. Although Bernardo had his own porter's lodge from which to watch the comings and goings of students and staff, he was much too restless to be content with sitting still all day, watching the world go by. He was fascinated by the science laboratories below the family's apartment. He spent many mornings and afternoons preparing them for experiments and cleaning up afterwards.

But, for Victoria, his most romantic task was that of night-watchman. 'If I was still wide awake, he would take me with him sometimes. All the lecture rooms and corridors which had been so busy and noisy during the day were dark and silent at night. It was a great adventure for me, but I wasn't afraid with my hand in his. Sometimes he woke me up early in the morning so that we could watch the sunrise from the roof. It was magic, pure magic. Once he took me into the university Observatory. Now that was a thing of wonder—a vast, glittering Aladdin's cave.

'Other children's fathers had one job each, if that. My father's versatility filled me with awe. Once I told him that there was nothing he couldn't do. He said. "No, Victoria, you are the one who can do anything. Anything. It's enough that you should want to do it. That is the knowledge which keeps me going, and never forget it. You are the best."'

Did Victoria's parents then know already that she was in some way 'special'? At first it seems possible, for she was afforded an extraordinary degree of protection. She was never allowed to help with the cooking and cleaning like her elder

6

sister Carmen, who was as outgoing and sociable as Victoria was withdrawn and shy. But a more credible and less romantic explanation of the manner in which she was shielded lies in Victoria's state of health. As a child she was distressingly thin and weak. If there was any extra food, Carmen kept back her share for her younger sister.

'It made me feel very guilty, sometimes, not being able to help my mother about the house when everyone else was being so busy, but it was absolutely forbidden. Sometimes when everyone was out I did some very fast tidying up. It was a sort of naughty indulgence just to do some real work for once.'

This over-solicitous protectiveness undoubtedly contributed to Victoria's shyness and her sense of isolation. Perhaps it was only the presence of the other young, talkative people at the university which prevented her from becoming wholly self-absorbed and introspective. Her father was fiercely proud of the place and popular with both staff and students. He had an uncanny facility for discerning the area and even the village of origin of new students by their accents, and thus establishing a rapport with them as soon as they arrived. And he never forgot their names.

'In later years, when I was touring the world,' says Victoria, 'I was astonished by the number of former students who would come backstage to talk about him. He had an enormous following.'

In the long summer vacations, the López children had the run of the university. In the humid nights of high summer, they were allowed to sleep out on the stone balconies under the stars. During the days, the balconies served another purpose. The children strung up a curtain at one end and improvised flamboyant plays. Victoria's happiest memories are of the gardens where once her father had worked. They were beautifully kept, and so large and secluded that it was like having their own private park. There was even a fountain in which they bathed when no one was looking.

'The trouble was', Victoria smiles, 'that somebody usually *was* looking. A married couple had been given charge of the

7

gardens. Their rooms overlooked our fountain. They disliked children and were always lying in wait to chase us off. "Get out!" they would yell. "Run along home!" And we would scream back, "Ogres, ogres! Mr and Mrs Ogre!" If they looked like catching us, we would scamper back home by the rooftop. But it was only to lay plans for a return visit to outwit them.'

Victoria and Pepe became voracious readers and enjoyed the same books. They developed an intense curiosity about the university library. It contained many rare manuscripts and first editions and was therefore strictly out of bounds to children. This, of course, only made them more determined to get in. Eventually they found a grille through which they could squeeze, and settled down, excited by the prospect of discovery and delighted by the thousands of beautiful books.

'But we grew careless and complacent as time went by. We went there once too often. One day we were sitting there, totally absorbed in our books, when we heard the deep voice of one of the senior lecturers only inches behind us. "Good day, scholars, and *what* are you doing in here, pray?" I think he was quite amused, but at the time we were terrified. Of course, Father was told, the grille was sealed and we never got back inside again.'

Bernardo feigned displeasure at this incident but was secretly delighted. He encouraged his children to read as much as possible. He himself read voraciously and had a simple man's admiration for all learning. For all his experience with students, he still regarded the learned as a favoured race apart. One day he returned home in high excitement with a hefty volume under his arm. He presented it to Victoria with due solemnity. She unwrapped it impatiently, expectantly. Her hopeful smile vanished.

'But, Father, it's a book on chemistry!'

'A very important book on chemistry. It's written by Professor Deulofeu downstairs. You must read it.'

'But, Father . . .'

'The professor has written it. Read it from cover to cover. We know the author.'

8

2

Victoria's formal education began when she was five years old.

'The whole idea of school was a nightmare to me,' she recalls. 'I hated the very thought of being shut in. I still do, as a matter of fact. Discipline and regimentation come very high on my shortlist of the unbearable. Also, of course, I was painfully shy. Just to say "hello" to another child was an ordeal. The most basic form of communication cost me hours of agonising and fear.'

Again, Victoria was lucky. A conventional school could so easily have turned her timidity into self-absorption and her loathing of discipline—the very mainstay of old-fashioned schooling—into sudden resentfulness. Discontent with the old schools, however, had recently caused the Catalan administrators to make a thoroughgoing study of the most advanced schools in Europe. The result was the foundation under the pre-Franco Republican government of the Grupo Escolar Mila y Fontanals. It is still regarded as a modern and exceptionally liberal discipline. In the five years during which Victoria was a pupil, it must have been way ahead of its time.

'We had wide open rooms', she remembers, 'and we worked on flat round tables instead of the usual school-desk. They

9

encouraged us to practise and appreciate all the arts. We did everything from music to pottery. There was a fine library where we could help ourselves to as many books as we wished. Pepe proved to be a very clever boy and went on to study in very much stricter circumstances under the Jesuits.'

But for all the relaxed informality of Mila y Fontanals, Victoria remained withdrawn. She preferred to stay indoors reading while the other children played and fought in the schoolyard. Her sister Carmen, a popular tomboy at the school, tried to draw her out, but without much success.

'Oh no, I was far too solemn, I'm afraid. Once, I remember, we were walking to school and a large, round lady in front of us suddenly slipped and toppled over. Carmen let go of my hand and ran over to have a look. I saw her shaking with suppressed laughter, and as soon as we were out of earshot she doubled up in fits. I just stood there, unsmiling and disapproving. Soon afterwards, when we were at home, I saw my grandmother, who was also large and round, fall over. I rushed up to her full of tears and alarm. But she was lying there, rolling from side to side and roaring with laughter. The harder it was for her to get up, the more she laughed—and the more I cried.'

Victoria eventually freed herself from the crippling bonds of shyness through her music. She had always enjoyed singing, and volunteered to be a member of the school choir. Singing with others was a liberating experience, and gave her a sense of companionship with her peers such as she had never known before. This in turn gave her the courage to holiday with the choir in the cool of the mountains behind Barcelona during the summer vacation.

There were regular concerts at these musical retreats. A particular friend had heard Victoria sing and had admired her voice. When a popular Catalan song with a fine solo part was to be performed, she urged Victoria to make a bid for the solo. On-the-spot auditions were held, but Victoria was too scared to push herself forward. To her friend's dismay, she was given neither that, nor any other passage to sing at the concert.

'You shouldn't just be a member of the chorus,' she said. 'You are better than that. Sing very loud, so loud that they have got to pay attention to you.'

Victoria did the very opposite, and proceeded to indicate her disappointment by failing to turn up at all on the day of the concert. She was to become one of the world's greatest prima donnas, but that was the first and the only time that she ever behaved like one.

For all that she enjoyed her singing, however, she had never even thought of it as anything more than an agreeable hobby. In so far as she ever thought of a career, she thought to be a doctor or perhaps a writer. Although it was a point of pride that she should excel at a school concert, she became increasingly reluctant to give the impromptu fireside concerts that her father so often insisted upon. With paternal enthusiasm he would coax her to perform.

'Now, you must hear Victoria sing. Come along and sing for them, Victoria.'

His pride was touching, but these ordeals became hateful to her. Maybe the visitor did not even want to hear her sing. Every parent in Barcelona believed that his child was a prodigy of one sort or another, and such displays were both inevitable and embarrassing. In Victoria's case the enthusiasm and persistence of the audiences overwhelmed her.

In those early years, Victoria did not play the piano. If she accompanied herself at all it was on the guitar. Then one day Victoria and some school friends found their way into a damaged and disused room in the university. The roof leaked, and the rain dripped down directly onto an abandoned piano. The instrument was so badly damaged that only a muffled hum could be coaxed from it. Victoria, nonetheless, was to remember the piano when she began her music studies at the Conservatorio. Then every available hand was recruited to bear this battered prize up to the caretaker's flat.

The next step was to get it into working order. Victoria obtained her mother's consent for some of the family's precious stock of olive oil to be used. Something approaching a clear note emerged. Her enthusiasm was infectious, and the ever indulgent Bernardo remembered that he knew someone who knew someone who knew someone who knew about these things. The piano was professionally overhauled.

The origins of Victoria's interest in medicine lie in her father's chronic asthma. She was fascinated by the efficiency and apparent omniscience of the doctors who treated him at the university clinic. She saw many raw students arriving at the nearby Faculty of Medicine only to leave a few years later as doctors, acquainted with all the mysterious workings of the human body. There were few female doctors in Spain in the 'thirties, but Victoria had been encouraged by seeing one or two female medics at the university.

In July 1936, when Victoria was nearly thirteen, the Civil War broke out. The war at once increased her appreciation of medicine and diminished her chances of attaining medical qualifications. She saw countless victims of the bombing receiving and responding to emergency treatment and surgery. At the same time, conditions in the city deteriorated so far that Victoria's education began to suffer. She had just begun preparations for her *bachillerato* or Higher Schools Certificate. Had she fared as well as her teachers expected, she would have gone on to university and thence, with luck and a great deal of work, to the fulfilment of her medical ambition.

'But it was impossible to study properly during the war,' says Victoria. 'Everything was such a mess that I couldn't take schoolwork seriously. I just gave up. There was no point in trying any more.'

Victoria's work was just one of many enterprises which foundered in the bitter, fearful days of the Civil War. As always in internecine conflict, men were reluctant to be called to arms, knowing that they might be called upon to fire on friends. Shortages of food and fuel became so acute that it was no longer possible to organise the fair distribution of resources. The administrators too 'just gave up', and the citizens of Barcelona were forced to grasp whatever they could wherever they could and to hold it by force.

The bombing threw university life totally out of joint. The building was hit more than once. Every time that the alarm sounded, the López family had to come down from the rooftop to the relative safety of the basement. Victoria remembers how frightened and flustered her mother became on each occasion. It was a long way down to the basement, and she was in a desperate hurry to see them all safely under shelter. The family even wrote a song affectionately mocking her undignified descent.

As always, the survival of the family depended upon the resourcefulness of Bernardo López. There was no longer any question of finding supplementary work in order to buy food. The problem was finding any food at all. In a world where the black market was the only means of obtaining sustenance, Bernardo's charm and his many contacts were invaluable. His friendships with students, lecturers, fishermen and merchants ensured that if vital supplies found their way into the city, he was among the first to hear of it.

Victoria recalls one occasion on which the family could obtain no olive oil. Although a luxury in the north, olive oil constitutes an essential part of the Latin's diet. Throughout the town, in the clubs, the bars, and in the university itself he told the same story, 'We need olive oil. Does anyone know where we can find some? We only need a little. . . .' His every enquiry was met with a gloomy shake of the head.

Then one day an old friend on the university staff drew him to one side and, hushing him with a gesture, handed him a piece of paper. Bernardo managed to decipher the scrawl. It was an address in the dingiest area of the old port. He made his way there slowly, constantly checking that no one was following him, for his reputation as a survivor was already well known. He knocked on the door. As he waited, he was hailed and beckoned by a man in a nearby bar. It was another contact who had discovered a totally different source of the precious oil. Not wishing to disappoint either of his informants he bought oil at both addresses and staggered home with far more than his family could use. He gave a reserve supply to his wife to hide in a cupboard beneath the stairs,

13

and another bottle to a family of neighbours recently bombed out of their home.

No sooner had he disposed of the first supply than it seemed that all his friends were sidling up to him, giving him a nudge and indicating where olive oil could be found. There was nowhere to hide his stocks and he could not even give it away to friends who, a few weeks before, had been as desperate as he to acquire it. That was the way of the war. All or nothing.

Where Victoria's studies were concerned it was nothing. Happily, this was also the moment when her voice, although still untrained, began to keep her busy. A member of the university staff who had been present at one of Bernardo's detested command performances and who was also a member of the Red Cross insisted that Victoria should perform at Red Cross concerts to raise money for the wounded. He provided a smart black dress which seemed to Victoria the height of *chic*. 'A Red Cross concert *and* a black dress—what more could I ask?' Victoria laughs.

At the first concert in nearby Molins de Rey, Victoria was excited to find herself billed to appear along with a popular gypsy entertainer, Vianor. He immediately took an avuncular interest in the young and nervous singer. He calmed her, assured her that the audience would love her and told her, 'Just go out there and enjoy yourself.'

All the shyness and reserve which had crippled her throughout her schooldays evaporated in the warmth of the applause which greeted her as she stepped out onto the stage. She sang for half an hour. Vianor watched from the wings. Occasionally he smiled or clenched his fist in a gesture of encouragement. The audience too seemed to want her to continue and cheered her on. She sang for another half-hour. By now she was too absorbed in what she was doing to look at Vianor. Had she done so, she would have seen his expression changing: from nervousness to impatience; from impatience to anger. At last he marched onto the stage. The audience was bellowing for yet another encore. Between his teeth he growled, 'Get off, child, get out of here! It's my turn! Off with you!'

Victoria had had her first lesson in theatre rivalry. She had not intended to upstage an experienced performer, but she had found such relief in her singing, in the feeling of closeness which she had established between herself and so many strangers whom she would normally have avoided. She, and they, had been so transported, at once by her need for such appreciation and theirs for innocence and hope in a sordid, hopeless age that neither had known when or even how to stop.

Only years later would Victoria conquer her shyness in everyday life, and then only through an extraordinary effort of will. In the meantime, only that communication between the singer and the applauding crowd afforded her the sense that she belonged among other people and was not wholly isolated.

She became increasingly popular and found herself constantly in demand at the many concerts in the area. At last, some politically active workers approached Victoria's father and demanded that she should perform with her guitar in Olot. Victoria and her grandmother were duly borne to Olot's main square and left on the pavement armed only with the family's shared guitar. Eventually a stranger escorted them to a cinema where a local singer was to perform.

A comic film was showing. The audience was composed of screaming, unsupervised children. By now, bored with the film, they were fighting. In imitation of their progenitors, no doubt. The auditorium was hot and smelled like a public convenience. Victoria was pushed hastily onto the stage and instructed to play a popular number from a *zarzuela* by Serrano. The local singer shortly turned up and started to prepare his piece.

Victoria was mortified. When the singer waved his hand at her to indicate that she should start playing, she let the guitar slip slowly to the floor. There was a chorus of ragged catcalls. The singer's voice faltered. The workers hissed at her from the wings, 'Play!'

'I . . . no, I don't want to.'

'Go on!'

The singer once again attempted to begin his song, but

15

Victoria refused to play anything. Suddenly she was snatched off the stage and bundled into a dilapidated car, and she and her grandmother were carried away. Her fee for playing between films was food—lentils, beans, sugar, all desperately needed.

Only now did Victoria realise that, although she had always taken her music for granted, it was a matter of the profoundest importance to her; she could not, she would not be ordered to play as though she were some sort of musical automaton. She needed to prepare, and above all she needed to know that those who listened did so with love and enthusiasm. This innate sympathy with an audience doubtless accounts for Victoria's rare ability to communicate with a small, intimate audience at recitals.

In March 1939, Barcelona was captured by the Nationalist Army under Franco. The war was over on the 28th.

Slowly the university returned to normal. World War II was to start in September of that year and Spain was to suffer for her neutrality. She was isolated, often despised. The trading connections on which she had for so long depended were broken. But at least Franco's sturdy refusal to enter the war afforded children of Victoria's generation the opportunity to resume their schooling and to look to the future. Food was still scarce, and rationing was introduced, even as in the countries at war. This meant queuing for basic supplies, but at least life was gradually returning to normal.

Bernardo's first concern was that Victoria should sit for her *bachillerato* at the Instituto Balmes (where her name had been entered) as soon as the war was over.

She recovered lost ground in history, literature and other arts subjects once her studies got under way again, but an early disinclination to grapple with mathematics, coupled with her lifelong dislike for any form of discipline, now crystallised into a loathing for anything to do with figures.

'They used to give me problems like, "If it takes 20 men, working 5 hours a day, 3 days to dig a hole of 10 cubic metres, how long will it take 35 men working $3\frac{1}{2}$ hours a day to dig a hole of 37 cubic metres?" and I was bemused. I wanted to

16

know the answers to all sorts of questions which they thought silly. What sort of hole was it? Why were they digging a hole at all? How well did the 20 men get on together? What did they do for the rest of the day?' The question would remain unresolved but her imaginings took flight. Eventually, she was so much preoccupied with the nature and character of the hole, not to mention the men digging it, that the problem went by the board.

Alas, mathematics at the Instituto Balmes was governed by one of its most feared and cantankerous old masters, one Professor Chinchilla. He was renowned for his violent fits of temper and for his refusal to accept that everyone could not readily understand mathematics. A literal mind like Victoria's was incomprehensible to him.

Just as a horse already doing its best will lay its ears back and stop at the touch of the whip, so Victoria, confused and frightened, simply responded to Chinchilla's impatient brow-beating by a stubborn refusal to make any progress whatsoever.

Bernardo was never a man to give up. Through his university contacts, he arranged an audience with Chinchilla. Victoria sat trembling in the anteroom as her father exercised his renowned charm on the irascible professor. He emerged all smiles, 'The good professor would like a word with you, Victoria. Now, come along. He's not going to hurt you. He is very understanding. Victoria, come on! You are wasting the kind professor's time . . . Victoria!'

At last he managed to drive his struggling daughter into the great man's den. Victoria stood with her back against the door, gazing wide-eyed at the professor at his desk on the other side of the room.

'Now then, Victoria,' Chinchilla smiled unconvincingly, 'your father has very kindly consulted me about your studies. You are very lucky to have a father who concerns himself so much with your progress, aren't you?'

'I don't know anything.'

'Now, come along over here and let's see you tackle this little problem.'

'I don't know anything.'

'Come along, girl. I'll help you.'

'I don't know anything.'

The professor sighed. 'You realise, Victoria, that you will have to work very hard over the summer holidays?'

'My father doesn't believe in holidays.'

Chinchilla's patience snapped. He slammed his heavy fist down on the desk, sending papers flying. 'Out, girl! Out! Get out of here and stay out!'

That interview marked the end of Victoria's ambitions to become a doctor for, although she worked hard that summer, her results were so unsatisfactory that she was summarily dropped from Chinchilla's class. Then, as now, one to whom mathematics was a closed book had no chance of qualifying as a doctor.

*   *   *

Victoria was not the only member of the family with a natural ear for music. Her sister Carmen was similarly blessed and was not hampered by Victoria's diffidence. She was convinced that Victoria's voice must be trained.

Without telling their parents, the elder sister had led Victoria to the Conservatorio of the Barcelona Liceo. Carmen was convinced that, if once Victoria had an audition, she could not fail. She had been heard by Mercedes Plantada. The girls were greeted with amusement and tolerance. 'But,' they were told, 'I'm afraid that you really are rather too young. Why not wait until you're a little bigger and then come back—with your parents, of course.'

Doubtless they shook their heads and laughed at the romantic aspirations of the two little girls. Doubtless they forgot them within hours of their leaving the building. But Victoria was not to forget. She took them at their word, waited, and returned. At 15 she was accepted on her second visit.

3

'Very nice, dear,' the woman's voice sounded somehow worried. 'Very nice. Would you mind sitting down for a moment, dear? I'll be back in a minute.'

Victoria sat, but as soon as the older woman had bustled from the room, she got up again and paced the room. She was too nervous to stay still. She walked over to the magnificent concert grand and absently strummed a few notes. She flicked dust from the top and watched it rising and swirling in the shafts of sunlight.

It was August 1939, and Victoria had returned to the Conservatorio del Liceo to audition for admission that autumn. She had been presented to Dolores Frau, the Conservatorio's principal singing teacher. Born in Mallorca, Frau had had a distinguished career as a mezzo soprano and had sung under the baton of maestro Toscanini among others. Victoria held her in awe. When first she had opened her mouth to sing for her, all that had emerged had been a nervous croak, but Frau had calmed her. 'I remember that first meeting very well,' says Victoria. 'Dolores Frau must have been in her fifties by then. She was rather stout and had a lovely, kind face. I felt so insignificant in front of her that I could scarcely sing a note at first, but she just smiled and encouraged me with those marvellous, twinkling eyes, and I felt as though I were at home. I quite forgot to be nervous.'

But then, just as Victoria had been getting into her stride, Frau had suddenly interrupted, jumped up and rushed from the room with that worried, incredulous look on her face.

Victoria turned from the window as the door opened again. Frau ushered a distinguished looking man into the room. 'Now, Victoria, please don't be nervous. This is the director of our Conservatorio. He would like to hear you sing.' She turned to the man, 'I tell you, it's remarkable, quite remarkable. She's not yet sixteen and already the voice is *impostata*.'

Victoria had no idea what Frau was talking about, but it was clear that she was very excited about something. That did not help. Nor did the introduction of yet another Very Important Person. Once again, however, Frau gently and patiently overcame Victoria's fears. When she had finished, Frau launched into an incomprehensible torrent of words and strange names. 'You see?' she gabbled, 'Already it is *impostata*. She could be another Rosina Storchio, another Claudia Muzio. Never have I heard such a voice in one so young. . . .' Victoria listened, astonished and uncomprehending. At last the director managed to break into Frau's gabbled panegyric. He drew her to one side. After a whispered consultation, he announced that Victoria would be admitted to the Conservatorio that autumn.

Victoria was just sixteen when the course started. It was a six-year course, or at least it was intended that it should be a six-year course, but that was to reckon without Victoria's aptitude and Frau's devotion. During the war years, Victoria had been drifting, purposeless and directionless. Now that she had found a direction, she worked swiftly and assiduously. She had completed the entire course by the time she was nineteen—and had walked off with a medal into the bargain.

From the start, Madame Frau fussed over Victoria like a broody hen. Her conviction that she had a great singer on her hands never wavered. Her first concern was to build her pupil up. 'Some mornings', Victoria recalls, 'she would say, "Today we are going out for a picnic. It is very important that you should fill your lungs with oxygen and your stomach with good food." So we would take the tram up to Tibidabo and have a huge picnic out on the grass.'

Until Frau took her in hand, Victoria was as thin as a rake. Her abiding memory of the war years is of the pain of hunger and, even though the war was now over, food was still strictly rationed. If she was to become the great soprano of Frau's dreams, she was going to have to put on a lot of weight and take a great deal of exercise. The plump teacher lost weight as she walked the hills and pressed her rations upon her waif-like pupil. Victoria filled out and grew in strength.

The special treatment which Victoria was accorded outside the Conservatorio was repeated in the classroom itself as the thin, shy pupil began to make extraordinary progress. When Frau came across another pupil with a problem she would always tell her protégée, 'Come over here, Victoria, and show them how to do it. Come and sing this passage for us, dear.'

Victoria, still as shy as in her first days at her first school, obliged. But being teacher's Star Pupil did not win her friends. It certainly did not enable her to overcome her abiding problem of communicating with those around her. She had her first conscious experience of envy. It made her retreat a little further still into a private world of fantasy and of reading alone.

'Most of the other pupils', Victoria remembers, 'at least outwardly accepted having an exceptional talent in their midst. But there was one girl with a really beautiful voice who dug her toes in. She left the room when, for the ump-teenth time, Madame said, "Sing it as Victoria does. Do it as Victoria has shown you."

'Next time that girl with the beautiful voice said, "If López is going to be asked to sing, then I'm not going to."'

By the time Victoria was into her second and third years at the Conservatorio, pupils sometimes had to put up with 'López' whether they liked it or not. If Madame Frau was unwell, Victoria was deputed to take over the class.

The trouble was that Victoria, in her own way, idolised Madame Frau just as much as she did Victoria. In her young pupil's eyes not only was Frau a Very Important Person, she was also a Perfect Person—a Goddess. Little by little, Victoria grew up and saw her teacher as an ordinary human being with good and bad points like everybody else.

'I remember the first time the halo slipped,' says Victoria. 'Madame came into the class and said, "Tomorrow is my name day. I'm going to make a little list of the presents to give me. Can I put you on the list?" I did not want to see my idol come to this pass. It would not have been correct for anybody, but least of all for Madame.'

Then real disillusion set in because Madame was a little too warm-heartedly impetuous in reassuring her star pupil over the first crisis in her relationship. It occurred at the beginning of Victoria's second year. Fees had to be paid for the term ahead and on this occasion Bernardo López had not been successful in raising the money. Worse, a friend of the family who was considered an authority on singing, was asked to listen to her voice and pronounced it good but not exceptional. Her talents were not so special. They would be well advised to get her into a university course where she could lay more practical foundations for her future. Victoria, who had at least realised that the voice she used to take so much for granted was to be her salvation, was distraught. In tears she hurried to Madame Frau to convey her grief and alarm.

'Don't worry. Everything is going to be all right. I'll arrange everything. We won't charge you for your classes. My lessons will be free. You tell your father to come to see me.'

Victoria was overjoyed. She rushed back home to arrange the meeting between Madame and her father.

'It's a pity you cannot continue to let us teach her,' were the actual words Dolores Frau spoke when Bernardo López was duly installed in her room at the Conservatorio. 'It's a pity. She could have made a great career.' There was no mention of the waiving or even of the postponement of fees.

Victoria was stunned. Her whole world collapsed about her. She accompanied her father home again in silence and locked herself in the darkness of her room to come to terms with the fact that the teacher she idolised and whose encouragement had given her such joy could abandon her at this moment.

Eventually she made up her mind to discover *why* she had been let down. Madame explained, 'I had to think about it. You see I helped two singers before, a tenor and a soprano, who were in difficulties like you. Neither of them remembered me afterwards. I wanted to help you as well. But really I could not allow that to happen to me a third time.'

In the end, thanks to Bernardo López's ingenuity, the money *was* found, but the fact that Madame had been prepared to allow the star pupil to fall by the wayside left Victoria with a permanent sense of disillusion. There was no question of a quarrel. When Victoria's career got underway in Spain, Madame was of course always invited to the performances. And when the international career was launched she always said, 'I told you that you were going to be somebody. I told you.'

In the meantime, however, the incident had served to bring home to Victoria how vital singing had now become to her and that, however easy the course might seem to her, she could never take it for granted.

Madame Frau was not her only teacher. Professor Antonio Bosom taught her theory and Tonic Sol-Fa, while Professors Graciano Tarrago and Teresa Gracia taught her to play the guitar and the piano. These instruments were secondary to her singing, however, and Victoria's conviction that she simply could not ever hope to be a good enough pianist to make a career of it proved justified. She continued to study, but her end-of-term results at the piano dropped from the 'exceptional' to the 'acceptable'. It reflected her by now all-consuming passion for singing. If an opportunity arose for her to get practical stage experience as an amateur she seized upon it. Most of the students enjoyed themselves, as students will. Victoria, however, did not participate in the usual round of parties.

'When I wasn't singing', Victoria explains, 'I loved to be alone. All I wanted to do was to be by myself, to think and to read. I was neither a party-goer nor a party-giver.'

'You must remember, too,' she adds, 'that when I was a student, young people in Spain did not have the freedom to come and go as they do today, particularly girls. Even when they did come together for the fiestas that were held on Saint Day holidays, the bonhomie struck me as terribly superficial. I suppose it was because I suffered so much just trying to hold a conversation with somebody. It made me prefer to be on my own. It was probably just as well, because the career I was preparing myself for meant that I would spend half my life alone in hotel rooms in distant lands.'

Carmen, Victoria's sister, continued to try to draw her out. One of her ploys proved so successful that the de los Angeles career almost got off the ground before she had even completed her studies at the Conservatorio.

In February 1940 when Victoria was still only sixteen, Carmen said, 'Now, Victoria, why don't you enter the Radio Barcelona Competition?'

'What competition do you mean?' said Victoria, cautiously.

'*Los Tres Cosacos* Competition. All you have to do is put your name down and they will audition you. Then, if they like you, you'll be able to compete. If you win you get a prize and you sing on the radio. Come along and put your name down.'

Although Victoria was by this time passionately devoted to singing, she was reluctant to push herself forward. Carmen took the initiative once more by frogmarching her to the offices of Radio Barcelona, where they were given the formal procedure to be followed. '*Los Tres Cosacos*' was a brand of cognac which has long since vanished. Instead of recommending themselves relentlessly to listeners of Radio Barcelona, *Los Tres Cosacos* had taken the more interesting course of sponsoring a singing competition on the wireless.

Under Carmen's watchful eye, Victoria wrote her name down as a competitor. But instead of the name she used at the Conservatorio, Victoria López, she filled in the words Victoria de los Angeles. It must have caught somebody's eye. A few weeks later the sisters were invited to present themselves at Radio Barcelona studios for an afternoon rehearsal and an evening broadcast. They did so with particular trepidation.

24

Victoria elected to sing Mimì's first act aria from Puccini's *La Bohème*. This was an opera that she had been working on at the Conservatorio. For the cafe-canteen style studio pianist with a bored expression on his face and a half-smoked cigarette in his lips, Victoria was altogether too much. He ran his hands over the stubble on his chin in disbelief at her methods.

Although then still only 16, she approached the concert with the same care and attention to detail that she would give years later to a recital, whether it was in London's Wigmore Hall or New York's huge Carnegie Hall. She sang in rehearsal in a very low and quiet voice, keeping the full volume in reserve for the broadcast itself. The pianist chewed his cigarette in surprise that a competitor with apparently so little power should be entering at all. Victoria replied by requesting changes in his tempi and a generally more sensitive accompaniment.

If things had not gone well that evening she would have been given short shrift by the programme's link-man, a much-loved and experienced entertainer by the name of Pusinet. He had a very loud gong and never failed to silence a tiresome competitor by giving his instrument a sharp blow. Once Victoria had completed her rendering of '*Mi chiamano Mimì*', however, Pusinet was overwhelmed: 'Ladies and gentlemen, you have before you a future glory of Spain.' She won her place in the semi-finals.

This time Victoria chose another Puccini aria from an opera that her name was always to be associated with, *Madam Butterfly*. But there was a hitch. Before she could sing 'One Fine Day', Pusinet had to see her birth certificate since her contribution, this time, was for the final round of the competition. Only then was it discovered that Victoria was still under age. The rules of the competition admitted only singers of 17 or over.

Suddenly it looked as though all Carmen's efforts to give her younger sister confidence would come to nothing. But, astonishingly, the rules were solemnly altered. From now on the minimum age for entering *Los Tres Cosacos* competition

25

would be 16, not 17. Victoria went through the rehearsals with the same care and professionalism that she had insisted upon for the semi-finals. This time the seasoned pianist was more tolerant of her style of preparation. And this time she emerged as a prizewinner.

The reward in January the following year was a full-scale production in, appropriately enough, the Teatro Victoria, sponsored by the *Tres Cosacos* Cognac Company. This was Victoria's first-ever public appearance in a full-scale opera. It was the first time she experienced the excitement of taking solo curtain calls. It was the first time she had the thrill of being handed armfuls of bouquets. And it was the first time that she sang *La Bohème* in public, an opera that she was to sing all over the world and make an album of that would go down in recording history as one of the all-time greats.

'My name then', Victoria remembers, 'was so terribly long. It was Victoria de los Angeles López García to please both my father, Bernardo López and my mother Victoria García, who were in the audience that night. My mother was very happy and laughing. She said, "If only we had had competitions like this when I was your age, I would have been on the stage like you as a girl." My father was more cautious. He followed the radio competitions carefully. But on the night he said, "Don't think this means you still don't have to pass your university entrance examinations, my girl."'

In all the excitement of the stage performance itself, it would have been easy to overlook the financial results of the prizewinning. The prize itself in fact was one thousand pesetas, about £25 in the exchange rate of the early 1940s. It was not a fortune—but it was a welcome boost to a family who had lived from hand to mouth for so long. Victoria kept back for herself only enough to buy a score of Boito's opera *Mefistofele* in an arrangement for piano and singers. She was due to sing an aria from the work at her first end-of-term concert.

The back of the kitchen drawer where pieces of string had formerly been kept was now turned into the family safe for the deposit of Victoria's first earnings which were put entirely at the family's disposal. The prize itself was supplemented by some expenses-paid concerts and appearances on Radio Barcelona, where the *Tres Cosacos* prizewinner was paid 75 pesetas an engagement, twice a month. Earning 150 pesetas a month, Victoria now realised she was the one who could rescue her family from the difficulties of their poverty.

Victoria was beginning to be noticed, not only by Dolores Frau, who thought of her now as having the makings of an international singer. At any private or radio concerts she now gave, it could so easily have happened that a management with an alert eye for her promise, might have signed Victoria up with the idea of the instant promotion of a young prizewinning artist. There is no doubt that if that had happened her career would have developed differently. She had now reached the stage of knowing exactly how important her voice was to her and of desiring above all else to make a career in music with it. But she was still very young and needed the guidance of a sort of musical godfather who could protect her from the commercial pressures that opened up in the wake of the *Tres Cosacos* prize.

By a stroke of such good luck that in retrospect it seems an inevitable happening, just such a person was in the audience of one of her end-of-term concerts at the Conservatorio.

4

End-of-term concerts at the Conservatorio were not renowned for respectful, appreciative audiences. Proud families turned up, sometimes three generations strong, to cheer their favourites on. Every time someone new stepped onto the stage, a small section of the audience stirred, and some mothers even prompted their offspring in atonal stage-whispers. Of course there were many family friends who came along and applauded, but these enthusiastic members of the audience were hissed into silence by the jury.

On May 14, 1941, José Maria Lamaña sat at the back of the hall. A thin, dark girl called Victoria López was singing the part of the Messenger in Monteverdi's *Orfeo*. Lamaña listened carefully. He leaned forward, his forearms on his knees, his hands clasped. His black double-breasted suit looked oddly mournful amidst the motley 'Sunday-best' around him.

As soon as the concert was over, he stood and walked resolutely through the departing crowd to the stage. He presented his card, and asked that it should be taken to Dolores Frau. The card bore the simple legend *José Maria Lamaña, Industrial Engineer*. Accurate enough, for Lamaña was indeed a distinguished engineer, and held an important position on the Spanish railways. But the card gave no

29

indication as to why Frau bustled out so promptly to greet Lamaña. For years now, he had worked on the railways only in order that he might indulge his ruling passion, music.

Frau already knew the name Lamaña. José Maria's father had been president of the Conservatorio many years before, and Lamaña junior held many honorary positions at the school. Among several other musical enterprises, he had founded in 1935 a successful seven-piece chamber ensemble called *Ars Musicae*.

He congratulated Frau on the attainments of her pupils, and particularly those of Victoria López. He was convinced that she could be a successful singer if only she were managed properly. Frau was delighted. She had Victoria summoned from backstage. Victoria remembers clearly her first meeting with this mini-Maecenas. 'He can only have been forty or so, but he seemed incredibly ancient to me. He had a high brow and was almost totally bald, which made him look older. His bearing, too, was that of a distinguished elder citizen, very *ancien régime*. He dressed very soberly, very correctly, always in dark double-breasted suits and stiffly-starched shirts with glossy collars and cuffs. I never saw him without a tie, even at home. His one concession to informality there was to replace the suit jacket with a cardigan.'

As for Lamaña, he saw a rather frail-looking child with large dark eyes who was just beginning to acquire prettiness. She came out in her one good dress. It was of dark green wool. It had a double row of pockets on the bodice and a pleat at the front. All were assiduously pressed every evening before bed. The neckline plunged rather daringly, and Victoria always wore a decorous silk scarf underneath it. She wore her first pair of high-heeled shoes which, of course (for they must serve many purposes), were still 'sensible' shoes with laces.

Carmen had recently taken her black hair in hand. It was now shoulder length and, thanks to her sister's attentions, curled softly at her forehead and her shoulders.

For all her pleasure at seeing her protégée congratulated by so discerning an amateur, Frau was an astute woman and a professional. She drew Lamaña aside and told him of her fears. 'Her parents are not well-off,' she said, 'And, as you can see, the poor girl gets nothing like enough to eat. I am always afraid that she might fall ill, and damage or even lose that magnificent voice. The other thing, of course, is that, even should she remain in reasonable health, she will inevitably be forced to take on unworthy commercial work simply in order to survive. That voice, Señor Lamaña, was made for better things.'

Lamaña agreed. He immediately proposed that he should advance to Madame Frau a monthly sum which would supplement Victoria's Conservatorio grant whatever might happen. What was left over was to be spent on milk, eggs, cheese, fruit, and any other supplements to her diet which Frau might deem beneficial. Frau accepted without hesitation.

It was arranged that Victoria should sing and play the recorder with *Ars Musicae*. This would at once give her experience of live performance and acquaint her with a wide variety of great and sometimes rather recondite music.

'We were very soon dubbed "Snow White and the Seven Dwarfs".' The dwarfs were, in fact, two women and five men of perfectly normal size. Between them they could turn their hands to twelve or more chamber instruments. 'One of them, Graciano Tarrago, had taught me the guitar at the Conservatorio. Another, Otto Schwarz, was a printer. The programmes that he prepared for our concerts were works of art in themselves.

'Lamaña was very severe, as a mentor must be. He used to take me painstakingly through each programme. He gave me detailed commentaries and long reading lists in order that I should have an insight into the period of each work's composition. He spoke in a very measured, considered, orderly way. One particularly humid afternoon, I remember, he had a whole battery of fans keeping the air moving. Their droning made me drowsy. I could feel my eyelids drooping. I struggled to stay awake, but the next thing I knew was that Lamaña was tapping my shoulder and it had grown dark. I had been sleeping for some time, but he had just carried on talking, totally absorbed, as though nothing had happened.'

Lamaña had the ideal combination of musical scholarship and practical experience in music-making to provide Victoria with a formidable higher education in music. He had studied for six years with one of Spain's leading musicologists. He had worked as secretary to a major orchestra. He had played trumpet in concerts of jazz and light music, and double bass in classical concerts. His erudite commentaries did not remain in an academic limbo. Each was applied in practice by *Ars Musicae*.

Above all, Lamaña was an indefatigable collector. *Ars Musicae* possessed a library of scores which would not have disgraced Alexandria. There were over a thousand for violin and piano alone. Lamaña had also amassed hundreds of ancient instruments or museum reproductions of them, so that the ancient music of Spain could again be played on the instruments for which it had been written.

Originally, *Ars Musicae* had given concerts in one another's homes and had performed the standard repertoire of the chamber ensemble. Increasingly, however, they were devoting their attentions to the revival of native Spanish music, a cause already championed by Manuel de Falla, who, concerned lest Spain should forget its own musical traditions, had organised whole festivals devoted to the performance of early music.

When not working, Victoria found the Lamañas to be warm and welcoming friends. They have remained so. Victoria was to sing in the church when their daughter, Maria Nieves, was married. Even now, in the 1980s, José Maria's wife Lolita is an enthusiastic visitor to every concert and opera performed by Victoria in Spain. Lamaña himself no longer makes long journeys, but Victoria telephones him frequently, and still consults him over the choice of programme when there is to be a recital of Spanish music. He retains a huge collection of photographs and cuttings from the early years of her career and a copy of every recording that she has ever made.

Victoria often joined the Lamañas in their airy apartment in central Barcelona for the long, mid-afternoon lunch which is the traditional focal point of Latin family life. She sat next to Maria Nieves, and, as the maid brought in course after course, Lolita regaled them with a constant flow of stories and laughter; 'If José Maria was reserved,' says Victoria, 'Lolita was always the very opposite. She existed on an outgoing tide of warmth. Do you know, she once got so enthusiastic at a concert of mine that they had to ask her to keep quiet!'

Lamaña was successful and well off, but he was not rich. His resolution that Victoria should complete her training was matched only by his resolve that Maria Nieves should not suffer for the sake of his protégée. He had no intention of allowing Victoria to sing for money until she was ready. The preparation of a great voice is like the honing of a blade. If the initial work is well and patiently done, the blade will need only a little stropping for it to retain its keenness. If the initial work is hasty and careless, no amount of work in the future will make it efficient. Victory in the *Tres Cosacos* had brought in countless offers of work which, if accepted, would have earned a reasonable income for the young singer. But Lamaña was aiming high. Victoria was to be a great opera singer and recitalist, not merely a good all-round singer. She needed the security to be able to say 'No' to all offers.

Some eighteen months after he had first heard Victoria sing, Lamaña sent out invitations to a handpicked group of Barcelona aristocrats and industrialists. The Pleasure of their Company was Requested at a concert to be held on December 13, 1942, in the home of Don Francisco Pons y Pla. He had chosen this address because its luxurious furnishings would provide an apt setting for the young singer and included a magnificent organ. The programme was entitled, 'The Oratorio and the Cantata in the Seventeenth and Eighteenth Centuries.' It included works by Carissimi, Scarlatti, Handel and Bach. An ambitious programme for 'Snow White and the Seven Dwarfs', perhaps, but the programme gave no other indication that this concert was to be a showcase for a brilliant young soprano.

The concert went well. Lamaña bowed graciously in response to the effusive compliments showered on his new discovery. Yes, she was impressive, wasn't she? Of course, it would take some time, but he believed that she had the makings of a really great singer who could bring glory to

Barcelona and to Spain. But alas, he could not raise a private scholarship, it would all go to waste. . . .

Five members of the distinguished audience got the point and volunteered funds for Victoria's training. Each, it was agreed, would contribute 500 pesetas (£11.23 at the exchange of the day) per month. There would be no conditions, and the money would be forthcoming for as long as it might be needed. To the monthly sum of 2,500 pesetas, *Ars Musicae* added a further 1,000 pesetas. Her total allowance was thus fixed at 3,500 pesetas (£78.65).

The group of five was called *El Patronato*. Their contributions were to be held and administered for Victoria by Lamaña. 'It was thrilling,' says Victoria, 'but I was instantly placed in a terrible dilemma. *El Patronato* wanted to set me up in an apartment of my own in a smart quarter of the city. Somehow they felt that because of my voice and its promise I no longer belonged in the class into which I was born. But I couldn't even consider leaving my parents and my brother and sister.

'In the end, we solved the problem by turning the main living room of the caretaker's flat at the university into my studio. It was redecorated throughout in white and looked very nice. Eventually *El Patronato* presented me with a beautiful Steck grand piano which stood in the centre of the room. It made it seem a lot smaller, but I was so, so happy there. I had my own studio, but I didn't have to be separated from my family. I had security, I had friends, and I had a sense of purpose, I could feel my voice growing stronger and richer all the time. I began to believe in the dreams of the others. As for the piano, I have never been parted from that. I took it with me when I married and again when we moved in 1968. It's my link with my first studio in my first home.'

With the much-needed sponsorship at last at his disposal, Lamaña now moved fast. Half of Victoria's allowance was passed on to the López family so that there should no longer be anxiety about food. The other half was paid in fees to the very best teachers who were to rehearse Victoria for her professional debut.

Mercedes Llatas, one of the *Ars Musicae* 'dwarfs' was appointed piano coach. Graciano Tarrago, the guitar teacher at the Conservatorio, now gave Victoria private lessons on an instrument that would prove indispensable if her recital programmes were to include the many traditional Spanish works which she had learned with *Ars Musicae*, and she was sent to learn German at college so that she could understand *Lieder*.

But the most important and the most controversial newcomer was the conductor and composer, Napoleone Annovazzi. He was appointed for a few months to prepare Victoria for her opera repertoire. Dolores Frau, however, remained her singing teacher, and Victoria found herself at the centre of a battle between two stubborn authorities with markedly different views. The rows between a man accustomed to commanding symphony orchestras and a woman whose voice had been trained to fill La Scala could be heard for miles around. Annovazzi maintained that Frau was training Victoria to be a *dramatic* when in fact she was quite clearly a *soprano lirica*. Frau claimed that, since she had been the first to spot Victoria's potential, it was up to her to decide how to train her voice.

But Annovazzi stood his ground. He refused to prepare her voice for those roles which called for the dramatic sort of soprano. He coached her instead in the lyrical roles of the Countess in *The Marriage of Figaro,* the title role in *Manon* and Mimì in *La Bohème.* His discerning ear and his stubbornness were triumphantly vindicated, for these were the very roles which were to win international acclaim for Victoria in the next few years.

The *Ars Musicae* concerts, meanwhile, gave the young singer a firm grounding for her recital career. The concerts were given in private homes, so there was no call for first night nerves. No public exposure was involved, and the press were not invited, but these concerts gave her a sense of purpose. They were a reward and a release after the many hours of long, monotonous work. She could do what she most liked to do—sing to an audience, and they rewarded her with applause and kind words.

Victoria describes her years with *Ars Musicae* as her

'university years'. She was sheltered, she was secure, she had time to think and to acquire self-awareness. At the same time, she learned both the theory and the practice of her art. Many other Catalan singers subsequently joined *Ars Musicae* for long and short periods to widen their experience and broaden their talents.

*   *   *

The voice was not the only property with which Lamaña concerned himself. If Victoria was to be a great artist and a true professional, she must acquire the self-discipline which the paying public has the right to demand. One infuriating trait which Lamaña battled to conquer was her total inability to be punctual for anything. Before every concert, Lamaña and the members of the ensemble would sit nervously fidgeting and glancing at the clock. Only at the last minute, when the audience, too, was becoming apprehensive and the musicians were resigning themselves to having to play an entirely different programme would Victoria breeze in. She was terribly sorry, but she had no watch.

Lamaña took the first possible opportunity, her eighteenth birthday, to present her with an excellent watch, but Victoria continued to arrive at the last minute, if not actually late. Lamaña was ruthless in his denunciation of amateurs and silly little prima donnas who could not be bothered to turn up on time, and Victoria would cry and ask his forgiveness. But it continued to happen.

'I cannot live with one eye always on the clock,' says Victoria ingenuously. 'Anyhow, do you know, in over thirty years of travelling the world, I've only ever missed three planes, and one of those does not count because the loudspeaker system at Heathrow had broken down so we didn't hear the last call even though we *were* waiting. Worrying about the time just isn't my way of living. It seems such a waste of time.'

Lamaña may have lost that battle, but there was another,

36

more serious problem ahead. This time he had to win, or all his other efforts would come to nothing. Victoria found the committing to memory of words and music very difficult. But, being a headstrong adolescent girl, that wasn't how she phrased it to Lamaña. She would not learn her music by heart. Why could she not read the score as orchestral musicians do? Lamaña was adamant. She would learn to learn or she could give up any idea of being a singer. The reason why Victoria had difficulties was the sheer profusion of scores she was given to study each evening. After a long day at the Conservatorio, further *Ars Musicae* lessons from 10 pm until 1 am or 2 am certainly taxed her strength as well as her memory.

Slight changes to Victoria's appearance were also suggested. Her dark hair was cut short, parted in the middle and worn in a simple classical style. She was equipped with a wardrobe of light summer dresses with short sleeves cut close to the shoulder. When she played the recorder with the group, she looked very young and frail. Soon a little sophistication was added by presents of jewellery; first a pair of pearl earrings, then a gold bracelet, then a single string of pearls —all very simple, all very understated. Victoria has retained that style throughout her life.

For all the work that had to be done, *Ars Musicae*'s attitude to music-making was far from solemn. They would try out songs dug up from their archives. Some were terrible, some surprised them pleasantly and they would take them into their repertoire. They would sing and play parody pieces and old favourite songs whose musical qualities, perhaps, were less obvious than the emotions that they evoked. Sometimes they got so carried away by the sheer exuberance of music-making that Lamaña would end up walking Victoria home at daybreak. She adopted the timetable which she keeps to this day. She goes to bed very late and rarely rises much before mid-day.

The group's work in preserving and reviving early Spanish music had earned them a reputation beyond Barcelona, and in late 1943, they received an invitation to perform at a small festival to be held at the Conservatorio in Madrid the following spring. Lamaña considered this an excellent opportunity to gauge the reactions of a wider audience to the group's protégée. He accepted the invitation, but arranged, too, that a little late-night recital would be given by a young soprano whom they happened to have with them. She would be accompanied by Mercedes Llatas, the group's pianist. She would also accompany herself on guitar.

So in March 1944, *Ars Musicae* gave two private concerts in Madrid before the most critical audience they had ever faced. In the first, Victoria played the recorder. She listened as part of the audience in the second.

It was a success. Afterwards, as a surprise for the guests, Victoria sang *'La maja y el ruiseñor'* by Granados, which was later to become almost the de los Angeles signature tune. A leading Madrid agent instantly approached Lamaña and asked that he might place her under contract. Otherwise, Lamaña was asked only one question, variously phrased, 'Why have we never heard of her before?' 'Where on earth have you been hiding her?' 'Who is she?'

Suddenly Victoria realised that the time for her professional debut drew very close. She could tell by the barely-concealed excitement and apprehension of her teachers; and Lamaña, while remaining a full-time engineer, was now playing manager. He arranged for many leading figures, including the impresario of the Barcelona Liceo, Juan Mestres, to come to hear her. 'We tried not to communicate our excitement and nervousness to Victoria,' recalls Lolita Lamaña, 'but I think we failed. We had been waiting so long for this moment. You must remember that we were, in effect, just a small group of provincial music scholars with a lot of hope and a firm conviction that we were right, but if we *were* right, we knew that what we were doing was going to affect the whole world. We were sometimes afraid that we had stepped out of our league. . . .'

Lamaña arranged for Victoria to make her first recording. This, of course, was the era of the 78 rpm. The record was made with His Masters Voice, then as now the most extensive and influential of record companies. Victoria's name was to appear beneath the famous motif of the dog and the phonograph for thirty years, but Lamaña had no thoughts of such a partnership at the moment. He was merely anxious that Victoria's voice should be heard abroad, particularly at HMV's head offices in London. She sang Lamaña's arrangements of 'Las majas de Paris' and 'La cancion de cuna'. HMV's director in Spain was sufficiently impressed to organise a second recording session.

The time had come. Everything that could be done had been done. Now it was up to Victoria. Lamaña meticulously drew up a list of entries in a ruled exercise-book. It was to serve as the record of his years as Victoria's manager. The headings were pencilled in: Date, City, Hall, Type of Concert, Director/Accompanist, Management/Agency, Takings. The first entry read: 'May 19, 1944, Barcelona, Palacio de la Musica, *Lieder* recital, Pedro Vallribera, Barcelona Association of Musical Culture, 750 pesetas.'

These bare facts reveal little save that the recital was held at the city's premier concert hall, that the 'seven dwarfs' gracefully stood down to make way for a professional accompanist (and a professional group, the *Cuarteto Iberico*), and that it was not particularly remunerative. *Ars Musicae* agonised for many nights over the programme. At last, they settled for works which spanned the full chronological range of classical music, from the high classical, through the romantics to the works of contemporary composers. Purcell, Handel, Bach, Gluck, Respighi, Brahms, Ravel, Loewe, Strauss and Victoria's coach, Annovazzi, were represented. The first notes that Victoria was to sing on the professional stage were from the recitative and aria from Purcell's *Dido and Aeneas*, an opera which many music lovers associate inextricably with the name of Victoria de los Angeles to this day.

'Everyone else was biting their nails and tearing their hair at the same time as they were telling *me* not to be nervous. But, you know, the extraordinary thing is that I wasn't at all nervous. I was still only twenty-one, and a very young twenty-one at that. At that age you do not carry the burden of the world on your shoulders. I knew, of course, that it was an important concert, but I didn't need to worry about living up to a name. I hadn't yet made one. I was just filled with a sort of youthful curiosity about the whole thing. While everyone else was suffering, I was out there enjoying myself.'

'After the debut', Victoria remembers, 'we all went from the Palacio de la Musica to the home of one of the *Patronato*, Mr and Mrs Alberto Par. There were champagne and canapés, and when it was all over somebody drove us home, my mother, my father, my brother and my sister. It was late by then and time to start another day.'

5

If the years with *Ars Musicae* were Victoria's 'university years', the first five years of her twenties were the years of apprenticeship. She was an acknowledged professional artist. Her commitments and her reputation grew throughout Spain. But she was still unmarried, still naïve and home-loving. Many evenings saw her leave the star's dressing-room with its flowers, good-luck telegrams, tributes and gorgeous costumes only to climb the stone steps to her little bed in the university's staff quarters.

Yet the pattern of her career during those five busy years was a scaled-down model of things to come. Just as, in later years, her world tours were to be organised around winter seasons at the Metropolitan in New York, so too her recital and opera engagements throughout Spain revolved about her winter seasons at the Liceo.

Few other singers have the good fortune to be born within walking distance of a great opera house. Victoria had already sung at the Liceo as a student of the Conservatorio, but opera-going had never been an activity of the López family. 'To me,' says Victoria, 'there was no particular mystique about the Liceo. It probably seems now that I was living in two separate worlds, one very glamorous and one very plain.

But after the civil war, even the Liceo was not very sparkling—certainly not when seen from backstage. Of course, there *were* very rich people who came lavishly dressed and wore lots of jewels for the big galas, but I always felt quite detached from them. I never envied them or held them in awe. In those days, you know, class distinction was very much more clearly defined. You belonged in high society, the middle classes, or, like me, the working classes, and that was that. You were no more discontented and resentful than a dog is discontented because he isn't a cat. I was the caretaker's daughter and I was at the Liceo because that was my place of work. I did my job and then went home. When I was at home, I simply knew, "This is my world. This is where I belong." I have never changed. If my parents were still alive and living at the university, I would still go home to them in the evenings as I used to in the old days.

'When the day came for me to make my opera debut, it all came to me quite naturally. I had done the rehearsals and they had all gone well. I felt that it was just a continuation of the singing I had always done. I do not mean to imply that I took opera for granted. But I never thought, "I must win tonight. I must conquer them." That was never my way of thinking. Why do you need to conquer? That means somebody has to lose. I had the voice and I loved the music so for me it was what it always had been—communication with others. I detest the idea of showing off, and I was not concerned with "making a success of it". I suppose I was not nervous because I was sure of myself and was not afraid of being ridiculous.

'Of course, it had all been prepared very carefully. I had been lent a mantilla and diamond earrings by a friend from the *Patronato*. My costumes were designed by Muntañola, a very good designer in Barcelona, who made them up as a present for me. I paid the seamstress who had actually put them together, but Muntañola insisted that his part in it should be a gift.

'There were no complimentary tickets for the Liceo first nights, so I spent lots of pesetas buying tickets for my family and their cousins and friends of theirs, all of whom wanted to come along.

'On the very first night of *Figaro* my parents headed the family party arm-in-arm. My father wore a dark suit that he had had tailored especially. He never dared to wear a dinner jacket. My mother wore a simple black dress.

'That evening my father made the first of his many tours of the aisles and the bars saying "hello" to everybody. He was not in the least intimidated by the crowds in evening dress and covered with jewels. He never had an inferiority complex because he was a caretaker or because he was a very short man. Because he was not in the least bit shy he was never inhibited by protocol which so often makes it difficult for one person to talk to another and say what they think.

'My mother's style was quite different from my father's. She gave the impression of being a very discreet person, I think. She used to hold that if there are some things that you don't know a lot about, it is much better to keep quiet and say as little as possible. She was always dressed very simply and unpretentiously and stood patiently at my father's side as he made the rounds. After the performance was over, there was the first of a number of little parties that were held at Mr Lamaña's. And then it was time to go home to bed at the university.'

At the time of her debut, the sumptuous, three-thousand capacity opera house was administered by Juan Mestres. He was a close friend of Lamaña, and soon the two men were filling in column after column in the manager's exercise-book. On January 13, 1945, Victoria would sing the Countess Almaviva in *The Marriage of Figaro*. There would then be a short season from January 17 to February 12, during which she would perform the other roles in which Annovazzi had coached her, the title role in *Manon* and Mimì in *La Bohème*. Both were to be key roles in her opera career.

Mimì had been in Victoria's repertoire since she won the *Tres Cosacos* when she was seventeen. As for Manon, the sixteen-year-old sybarite seeking to escape the boredom of convent life, any young singer might be expected to sympathise with Massenet's heroine. But how could Victoria, an inexperienced young woman of 21, convincingly convey to an audience the terrible passions of the Countess Almaviva, her debut role, who is tormented by her husband's insane jealousy and his blatant infidelity and, at the last, forgives him in passages of incomparable nobility and tenderness?

'Instinct', says Victoria, 'instinct and that incurably romantic nature of mine. When you are very young, you have the courage and the spontaneity necessary for a part like that. Somehow you just know how to do it without all the reflection and analysis of later life. Mozart does most of it for you, anyhow.'

Mozart and Victoria did very well between them. The critics and the public praised the new resident star unanimously. The managerial exercise-book records that the 1,000 peseta fee for the first performance had been raised to 2,500 for the last in February.

'At the Liceo', she recalls, 'I really sang exactly as I wanted. Apart from the essential moves onstage, nobody told me what to do at all. I had never seen the works performed, and there were no great international singers coming to perform in Spain so soon after the war, so there was never any question of my modelling my performance on any other. I was lucky, too, in that I had the freedom to work on my own without any star conductors or directors to lay down the law. I think that when you are very young and inexperienced you can be destroyed by people who treat you like a puppet. They want you to be an extension of themselves rather than allowing you to find yourself in your role. I mean, I sing women's roles, written for women singers by some of the greatest and most sensitive artists who ever lived. There is much of Almaviva, for example, in me. I must find it and respond to it, rather than having a man, however fine a musician, tell me, "No, no, she would express herself *so*."

'Once I had completed my course at the Conservatorio with Dolores Frau, I never had another singing teacher. Other singers, I know, continue to work under masters for much of their performing lives, but I believe that a professional should be her own teacher. So I went to the opera house with the parts completely prepared. I simply could not bear the

44

thought of a *répétiteur* hammering out the rhythm and destroying all the insight into a role that I had acquired. I just locked myself away with the words and the music and lived with the character. I hate to think of the rows there might have been had I started my career in less fortunate circumstances.'

Until 1949, Victoria was the Liceo's resident star and hard-working repertory artist. The part of Marguerite in Gounod's *Faust* was another which was to prove one of the mainstays of her operatic career. The management paid her the compliment of engaging French artists for the French operas and Italians for the Italian operas. Eventually, too, she was given German roles, notably the Wagner heroines, Elisabeth in *Tannhäuser* and Elsa in *Lohengrin*. She soon became accustomed through these roles to representing goodness and virtue. Luckily, the devil did not have all the good tunes. Another notable Liceo debut was the triple bill of Monteverdi's *Combattimento*, Wolf Ferrari's *Segreto di Susanna* and Pergolesi's *Serva Padrona*—given all on one evening at the Liceo and repeated for Victoria's Lisbon debut.

As for the excitement which attended this first stage of her career, Victoria resolved that, for the time being, she would cut herself off from it completely and live just for her music.

She found that she took quite readily to the huge, extrovert audiences that fill a great opera house like the Liceo. She had until then been accustomed to the smaller, more dedicated and critical audiences of the home recitals. It could sometimes be difficult to capture the attention of the opera house audiences, let alone their hearts, but Victoria now remembers the public of those years with affection, 'They were tremendously loyal to their house artists.'

Lamaña knew that Victoria's reputation could not rest solely on her triumphs in Barcelona. She must travel further afield and conquer new territory. The war was over now, but it was far too early to expect much musical activity in war-ravaged Europe outside Spain and Portugal. Madrid and Lisbon must, therefore, be her first targets.

In 1945, the 620 kilometres separating Barcelona and

Madrid seemed far more daunting than they do now. There were no motorways, no fast inter-city trains and no air shuttles. So soon after the civil war, communications were antiquated and unreliable. On the journey to her first professional engagement in Madrid, therefore, Victoria had her first taste of living out of a suitcase and the endless delays of travel.

'In those days', she says, 'the journey to Madrid and then on to Lisbon took nearly three days. I read books and took up crocheting and knitting which my mother had taught me. I knew that they would not start without me, so I never worried if it took a long time. If you fret about travelling, you'll be no use at all by the time you arrive. I soon learned that it was best to try to arrive a day or two early so that I could sleep and walk around the place and compose myself before going on stage. I also learned never to get upset about hold-ups, even if they were due to inefficiency. It never does the slightest good.

'In those days, my mother always travelled with me. We must have been very strong. We used to sit upright all night in those very slow trains. If we slept at all on the overnight journeys, we dozed with our heads on each other's shoulders. Very often there were so many delays that we went straight from the railway station to the concert hall.'

Victoria may have regarded the prospect of late arrival with equanimity, but Julian Uceda, who ran the *Sociedad Musical Daniel* organisation in Madrid could not afford to be so philosophical. His organisation presented Victoria at the *Teatro Calderón* for her recital debut in the capital on March 5, 1945. When this, in turn, led to recital tours, his enthusiastic involvement and ingenuity helped to ensure that Victoria arrived on time, 'though usually by means of an elaborate combination of trains, ancient buses and lifts from friends. People then', says Victoria, 'seemed to have a tremendous sense of fun and great resources of patience. Now that we can all get about so much quicker, people often seem to be in a horrible temper because they cannot move even faster. You had to be content to take things easy in those days and to laugh at the delays.'

That recital debut brought such enthusiastic notices from the critics that Victoria would clearly be given the chance to make her debut in opera at the first opportunity. One reviewer recalled the great coloratura-mezzo Conchita Supervia, who had died in the 1930s, and trumpeted, 'At last, after all these years, Spain has found another great voice to give the world.' Another spoke of a young artist who promised to 'reflect great glory on Spanish music and on Spain.'

While waiting for the right moment to make her operatic debut in Madrid, Victoria returned there for a series of concerts in the spring and autumn of 1945 and 1946. That she was packing in the crowds and acquiring celebrity is clearly demonstrated by the fees that these recitals commanded. For the first, in 1945, she received 2,000 pesetas. By the time of the last in 1946, Lamaña's register shows that she earned 4,500 pesetas per evening.

In November 1946, Victoria began her long association with the Spanish National Orchestra, which was at that time conducted by the venerable maestro, Perez Casas. The irreverence, spontaneity and confidence of the young soprano is exemplified by an incident at her first rehearsal with Casas and the orchestra.

'We were rehearsing Ravel's "Kadish", and I was sure that the maestro had not quite got the tempo right,' she says, 'so I just raised a hand and said, "Excuse me, maestro Casas, but do you think I might borrow your baton for a moment?" He looked quite stunned, but he held out the baton all the same. Then I showed the orchestra the way I thought it should be done. I'd never dream of doing something like that nowadays, but I suppose that I was young, and I certainly had no intention of causing any offence. All that I wanted to do was to help. Anyhow, once he had recovered from the shock, Casas laughed and said, "Thank you, Madame Toscanini" and, in the evening, he duly followed my lead!'

In the spring of 1947 there arose the perfect opportunity for Victoria's Madrid debut in opera. One of the greatest tenors of all time, Beniamino Gigli, was to perform in Spain. Gigli's fame had continued to grow throughout the war years thanks

47

to his many recordings, but he had returned to Italy for the duration and only now had he emerged from the magnificient Villa Montance which he had built for himself in his native town of Recanti to resume his world tours. Victoria was singing Manon to his Des Grieux and Mimì to his Rodolfo. The performances were immediately sold out.

Gigli was 57. Although no one could have guessed that he would be dead within ten years, it was generally felt that there would be few opportunities to hear again the voice that had been thrilling audiences throughout the world since the 1920s, the voice which now earned him as much as, if not more than, any 'popular' singer of the day. It was conservatively estimated that Gigli earned £50,000 a year in these last few seasons of his career.

Following in the footsteps of Caruso, Gigli had been a resident star at the New York Metropolitan. De los Angeles was soon to occupy that position herself. It is tempting to see these Gigli–de los Angeles performances in Madrid as historic occasions on which the great senior artist passed on his experience and his mantle to the newcomer. It was not so.

'I'm afraid that we only met onstage. The first words exchanged between us were sung, not spoken. He was Des Grieux and I was Manon. By the time that we actually met offstage, any chance of a close constructive friendship was gone.'

At first, Gigli was generous. He even led the applause when Victoria sang the aria, *'N'est-ce plus ma main que cette main presse?'*, in which Manon persuades her lover to renounce holy orders and to come away with her again. But the applause needed no leading. The Spanish audience had discovered a great new singer and, what was more, she was their own! They were rapturous, and as she took her curtain calls the applause swelled. . . . They were stamping and shouting and throwing flowers, coats, jewellery, even, onto the stage —all of which was a little unseemly, considering that Gigli had thought this production to be a showcase for Gigli.

When they sang together for the second time, in *La Bohème*, the audience again stood to welcome their own rising star, but they waited in vain. Gigli took his curtain calls with the conductor.

'Apart from a performance a few months later I didn't see Gigli again for many years until he was in New York in the mid-1950s for his farewell at the Carnegie Hall. I was singing myself that evening, but I met him on 57th Street and I was so pleased.

'I called out to him, "Beniamino, how are you?". He looked at me for a moment and said, "Who is it?"

'"Victoria", I said, "Victoria de los Angeles."

'"I remember now", he said, "the girl with the lovely big eyes. I remember now."

'That was the last time I ever saw him,' says Victoria. 'I remember him as being very extrovert with the outgoing manner that marks so many Italian tenors like di Stefano and Tagliavini. Only Mario del Monaco was more reserved.

'I actually came to appreciate what fun the Italians could be in the occasional tours I made in the next few years in northern and central Spain. They were organised by a very enterprising couple who put all the artists on a bus instead of handing them individual rail tickets. It was less expensive for them to organise things in that way. And I did enjoy being on those old buses with all the company. The Italian tenors like di Stefano were there making everybody laugh and sing. My mother enjoyed it, too. For her it was like a wonderful holiday. A little bemusing, I think, but she entered into the spirit of it and looked after me so well on those first tours in Spain.

'When we got off the bus in a city like Bilbao, she would take me straight to the hotel. "Now you lie down and rest. You've a performance to do," she would say. "I shall go to the theatre and make sure your costumes are there and everything is all right with them." She became very experienced at it. She loved to be in the middle of the excitement. My father was not at all happy for my mother to be away from home for so long. He needed her there to look after the home. To be without wife *and* daughter, was too much. So he allowed my sister to come along, instead, for the next season.

'I used to write a lot of letters to my parents while we were away. Many years later, when they had both died, I came across a trunk containing all the letters that I had ever written. I never looked at them again. I destroyed them. It was a time that had been and gone.

'I sang a lot in those days, too, with Di Stefano—in Barcelona, Madrid and on tour in Spain. I think Di Stefano was the first of our generation to go to the Met. They told me that he talked a lot about me there, and they began to become interested in this young Spanish soprano in New York!'

The following year saw Victoria back in Madrid with the Italian and French roles that she had been singing during the winter in Barcelona. She then toured with all these roles, to Seville in the South, Valencia in the East, Oviedo and Bilbao in the North. She toured, too, with her recital programmes, taking in Lisbon, where she scored a notable success. Within five years, Victoria was recognised throughout the Iberian peninsula. Now was the time when she must find a platform outside the boundaries of her own homeland. Now, too, she had the chance, for life was returning to what passed, in post-war terms, as 'normal' throughout Europe. Good music was demanded by the public. Lamaña looked around, then selected a singing competition in neutral Switzerland as a means of introducing Victoria de los Angeles to the rest of the world.

6

'Of course, I am absolutely certain to win,' Victoria wrote to Lamaña from the little hotel above Lake Geneva. Then, 'Oh, if only that were true!'

For the first time in her career, Victoria was showing signs of nerves. It is not surprising. Until September, 1947, she had been a big fish in a very small pool, a peculiarly-gifted girl without peer in her homeland. But here in Geneva there were one hundred such gifted musicians from all over the world, each with the same sort of reputation among his compatriots, each carrying the hopes of patron and country just as Victoria carried those of *Ars Musicae* and of Spain. They had come to Switzerland to compete for a major prize, that of the *Concours Internationale d'Exécution Musicale de Genève*. There were to be two elimination rounds, on September 30 and October 1. The prizewinner would then give a concert at the Victoria Hall on October 5. The first prize, a mere thousand Swiss francs (£57.63 at the rate of exchange of the time), may seem paltry, but the attendant prestige was incalculable.

Others, too, had been apprehensive about Victoria's chances in the contest. So soon as Lamaña had suggested that she enter, timorous friends had argued against it. She had already established a considerable reputation as a recital

artist and as resident leading soprano at the Liceo. Why risk
the indignity of being passed over as an also-ran in an
international competition? Lamaña, of course, was sure that
there was no such danger. Victoria was by no means so
confident, but concluded that, at worst, the experience would
be useful.

It was one thing to decide to set off for Geneva, but quite
another to get there. First they had to raise the necessary
money to finance the trip, then find some means of overcom-
ing the tight currency controls which prohibited the export of
pesetas. Victoria was now a star in her own country. It was
ridiculous to expect *El Patronato* to sustain their already
generous support. Lamaña therefore decided to apply for
foreign currency. He wrote a long and persuasive appeal to
the appropriate government department, the *Instituto de la
Moneda*. He argued that Spain's once great reputation in the
world of music was now a tawdry, tarnished thing. Victoria
was better equipped than any other to restore it and to reflect
glory on Spain and Spanish culture.

His eloquence was wasted. Bureaucrats are always slug-
gish, and Latin bureaucrats doubly so, so it was some time
before the considered reply arrived on Lamaña's desk. There
was no question of financial aid. There was no question of
lifting currency controls. 'Yours' in comforting triplicate, etc.

But Lamaña had resolved that Victoria would not only go to
Switzerland but would go in style, as befits a *prima*. One of
his brothers at length volunteered the money. Then he
recalled that he just happened to have a distant relative who
had a not-so-distant colleague who had a close friend in the
Spanish embassy in Geneva. Currency controls were dis-
creetly side-stepped.

Not only, then, would Victoria take her chance at the
Concours, but it was arranged that she should fly. In those
days, passenger flights were for American millionaires or
V.I.P.s with urgent business. 'It was almost as exciting and
newsworthy as if I had been going to the moon,' Victoria
recalls. 'The flight which now takes just seventy-five minutes
then took three hours. I had a complete new wardrobe, and all

52

my friends came to see me off. All the press were there, too, more because I was flying than because of the competition, and I had to wait for ages while they took their photographs. Then it was up the six steps of the ladder and into what now seems a very rickety old plane.

'Then I really was nervous. Not only was it my first flight and my first major competition with top-class musicians, it was also the first time that I had ever made a journey on my own. It was just too expensive to send a companion with me, so Mr Lamaña had to stay at home with his fingers crossed.

'It was a wonderful experience, seeing Switzerland for the first time from the air; all the chalets and the lakes and the animals looked like toys in papier-mâché mountains. I very quickly forgot my apprehensions in the sheer exhilaration of it all. When we landed, of course, they all came flooding back. This was the big wide world, and I was taking it on, alone.

'I went straight to the Conservatoire to rehearse with the pianist, and discovered to my horror that I could not sing a single note. I was terrified. After all that excitement, I had lost my voice. I wouldn't be able to sing in the competition. Maybe I would never sing again! Of course, it was soon explained to me. In those days, you see, there was no such thing as depressurisation. Somehow, the flight had completely deprived me of my voice. I was told to go to my hotel and sleep. In the morning, I would be fine. For once in my life, I had an early night.'

She got up early the next morning, too. As she had been assured, her voice was once more in perfect working order. She wrote with increased confidence to her *Ars Musicae* friends, 'During this morning's rehearsal, they introduced me to the singer who, they said, would be my main rival. I must confess that I came out much happier than I went in.'

Until the first round of eliminations, there was nothing to do but to explore this new world. Switzerland's neutrality, of course, so far from serving her ill, had made her still wealthier than ever. The shop windows dazzled Victoria, and her letters are full of childlike, breathless wonder. 'If only I were a millionaire,' she wrote to Lamaña, 'I'd buy everything!' But limited resources largely restricted her to window-shopping. She bought stockings for her sister, lace for her mother, slippers for her father, books for her brother.

She also bought music. 'Oh, I couldn't resist it,' she smiles. 'I went on a wonderful spending spree in those music shops. I still have the scores that I bought then—Ravel, Duparc, Purcell, Mozart, and wonderful collections of traditional songs from Greece, Hungary and Czechoslovakia. In Spain it would have been impossible to find a wide selection of music like that. It was a treasure trove.' In another letter to Barcelona, she effuses, 'Just imagine, I found a complete score of Erik Satie's *Socrates*. Much, much too expensive, of course. Oh, if only I had lots of money!'

Victoria did have enough in her purse to buy herself a cup of chocolate but not the experience of freedom just to go into a café, sit down alone and order. 'I passed a beautiful old world café several times on my shopping expeditions and could see through the window the people were sipping hot drinks with cream piled on them. I just longed for some too. But I was much too shy to walk in and sit down alone. I wandered backwards and forwards passing the entrance trying to get up the courage to go in. Suddenly I dared to go in—and there I was, inside drinking hot chocolate. Now it seems like nothing, but for me then it was quite an achievement. Spanish girls just did not walk into cafés on their own in those days.'

At last the day of the first round arrived. Victoria was astonished by the way in which the competition was conducted. 'I suppose it was quite funny, really. The idea was that the jury should not know who we were or where we came from, so we were summoned by numbers rather than by names. When your number was called, you had to stand up behind a curtain and sing to the jury on the other side. So there I stood, projecting my voice and making expressive gestures at a thick, dark curtain, and feeling not a little silly!'

Bizarre as the conditions may have been, they do not seem to have affected either Victoria's skills or the jury's discernment. She was one of eighteen chosen to go through to the final on the following day.

In the first and second rounds, Victoria had performed songs by Handel, Monteverdi and Beethoven. For the final round, sung in the Victoria Hall in full view of the jury, she would include those composers' works together with a piece by Ravel. Victoria's spirits fell. Not only were there no Spanish works on the list from which competitors were to choose their entries, but a Czechoslovak soprano had made an evident impression on the judges with her interpretation of Wagner arias. Already she was widely tipped to win. The aria with which Victoria made the most favourable impression was an unlikely one, Leonora's '*Abscheulicher!*' from *Fidelio*.

As if to prolong the agony of the finalists, the results would not be announced until midnight. Until then, there was a grand reception. Victoria, still shy and decidedly overawed by the whole event, nonetheless steeled herself to appear.

A tall man strode up to her as she entered the room. In a quiet Teutonic voice, he congratulated her, brushing aside her protestations with, 'Come, come, my dear. After that "*Abscheulicher!*" there can be no doubt as to the winner.'

Victoria stammered her embarrassed thanks. 'But I think I'd have swallowed my tongue completely if I'd realised then that he was the director of the Salzburg Mozarteum.'

The strain of the day was beginning to tell. The small talk wearied her. She had no escort, so, with characteristic ingenuousness, Victoria simply decided to go to bed. She returned to her hotel and slept soundly whilst pundits and performers alike awaited the midnight announcement of the winners.

There was a banging on the door. Victoria turned over in bed and pretended that she had not heard it. Perhaps it would go away.

It didn't. 'Telephone for you, Mademoiselle.'

Victoria looked at her watch, *Ars Musicae's* present, which lay by her bed. Eight o'clock in the morning. It couldn't be Barcelona. They knew her too well even to think of ringing before midday. 'All right! I'm coming!' she shouted. She swung her legs off the bed. Then she remembered why she was in Geneva. The Competition. The winner had been announced last night, but she had heard nothing. She couldn't have won. She just shrugged. It didn't matter much. She was sorry, though, to have disappointed her friends. She picked up the telephone.

'Darling! I know I must be the ninety-third person to ring you this morning and you must be absolutely fed up, but I just had to ring and say it all the same. . . .'

Victoria recognised the voice. Her friend, Barcelona pianist Sofia Puche, was in Geneva at the time.

'Say what, Sofia?' asked Victoria, her brain still clouded by sleep.

'Why, congratulations on being such a clever soprano, of course.'

'And congratulations to you on being such a clever pianist. But why are we congratulating one another on our professions at this horrible hour in the morning?'

There was a very long pause. Then, 'You mean you don't even know?'

'What?'

'No midnight telephone calls? Fanfares of trumpets? You mean that you slept through the whole thing?'

'You mean . . .'

'I mean, my dear Victoria, that I have the historic privilege of informing you that you are the outright winner of the *Concours Internationale d'Exécution Musicale du Conservatoire de Genève*, that your name is in every paper and on everyone's lips and . . . and . . . congratulations!'

Victoria's first sensation was one of intense relief. 'Of course, I was pleased,' she recalls, 'but just longed to be back in Barcelona.'

But first she must give the winner's concert at the Victoria Hall. As the telegrams came flooding in from Spain, Victoria's homesickness grew. At last, it was all over. The concert was given and broadcast. She had talked to the press and received the acclaim of the experts and the public. She sat in her hotel room on the last morning. Her bags were packed. 'I was more excited to be going back than I had been to go out there in the first place,' she says.

(*Left*) Victoria with her elder sister Carmen and their father, on the balcony of their flat

(*Below*) The entire López family, including Victoria's brother José

(*Above*) As a teenager in the grounds of Barcelona University

(*Right*) Victoria with her father in his university porter's uniform

(*Left*) At the 'tres Cosacos' competition
(*Below*) Victoria's first public appearance

(*Above*) Walking in Barcelona with her singing teacher Dolores Frau

(*Left*) Triumphant 16-year-old prize-winner holding the 'tres Cosacos' cup

(*Above*) Victoria with the *Ars Musicae* group, playing the recorder with José

Maria Lamaña on percussion, and (*below*) a relaxed moment with Lamaña

A formal portrait to mark Victoria's
official debut at the Barcelona *Palacio
de la Musica* on May 19th 1944

(*Above*) Victoria as guest of honour at a
banquet in Barcelona flanked by
Dolores Frau and Antonio Par to
celebrate winning the Geneva
Competition

(*Right*) Victoria's parents always
accompanied her on first nights

(*Above*) Dining out after a performance at Covent Garden, with her husband Enrique (with moustache)

(*Opposite*) As Mimì in *La Bohème*, the role with which Victoria made her Covent Garden debut

(*Left*) Victoria with her Paris-based European manager, impresario Leonidoff

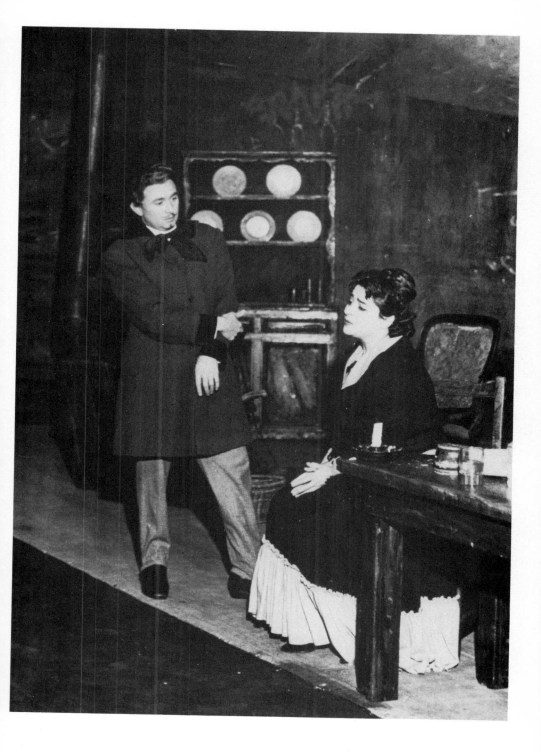

(*Above and left*) As Butterfly, the opera role with which Victoria most completely identified

Once again there came a hammering at the door. Once again she was summoned to the telephone.

'Hello. Miss de los Angeles? It's Oldani here of La Scala, Milan. Many congratulations.'

'Thank you so much.'

'We heard the broadcast. Magnificent. We would very much like you to come and sing for us here.'

'Oh, I'd love to, but I'm afraid I'm going home today. I've got my ticket here.'

'I quite understand, of course, but I am sure we can arrange something. It would only be a brief detour. You could change your ticket and fly back via Milan.'

'No, thank you. I want to go home. They're waiting for me.'

'Um . . . I don't think you understand. This is La Scala. We are asking that you come to sing for us at La Scala.'

An incredulous Oldani put down the telephone in Milan. Victoria was not playing hard-to-get. She simply wanted to return to Barcelona and there was an end to it. As for bookings at La Scala, such things were in Lamaña's hands. This flight had taught her that she must never again travel on her own and try to act both as manager and as artist.

Victoria had arrived in Geneva unheralded and unknown. She left amidst crowds of journalists and well-wishers. A state official was there to wish her godspeed and to express Switzerland's hope that she would return. But if the send-off was exuberant in reserved Swiss style, the welcome in Barcelona was in a different class for colour, noise and sheer joy. *Ars Musicae, El Patronato*, her family and friends awaited her at the airport with huge garlands of flowers.

'And when we got back to the university, it was unbelievable. I got the lift up to the top floor, and when I stepped out, I was just dazed. Everyone was there. The whole of our balcony was one great mass of flowers. There must have been a hundred bouquets. It was so good to be home.'

It is impossible to say how Victoria's career would have been affected had she accepted La Scala's invitation at that early stage. Luckily, La Scala was prepared to wait. What is certain is that, as far as Victoria was concerned, it was worth it.

7

Victoria had fallen in love for the first time at the age of 12. 'He was the son of one of the assistant porters at the university. And he never knew.' Remembered as a nimble, dark-eyed young man, he went about his business quite unaware of the admiration he had inspired. The romance was unspoiled by anything as mundane as meetings or having conversations.

'I think that it is very difficult', says Victoria 'for anybody growing up in the 1980s to appreciate what it was like to be a young girl in Spain in the 1940s. Teenage children I meet through my own family today seem to have made up their minds about all sorts of adult things we were quite ignorant of. We had no television, no instant sophistication brought by magazines aimed at the young. I think that young people today have to be so much harder because they are exposed to the nasty side of life so soon. They have to be so much more aggressive because they have to face so much violence. For me it was quite different. I was a very romantic person and I was able to hold on to my romantic conception of life because we were not always exposed to harsh and ugly things. We had a radio—but it only carried good news! If things were going wrong we were never allowed to hear about them.'

A few months after she had fallen in love with the dark-eyed young man, he moved away from the university and disappeared from her life. Not long after, however, somebody else came along to sweep her off her feet. In the basement of the university where the family had taken shelter during the bombing of Barcelona there was a students' canteen. 'It is still just the same,' says Victoria. 'The counter runs down one side, and on the other students sit and drink and talk at the top of their voices. Because it is underground it gets very smoky because there are only half windows at ceiling level for light to come in and for the noise to escape. Last time I was there I noted they still had the same little old cash register. Undergraduates still sit around there gossiping over a glass of wine or a coffee.' Victoria sometimes went in with her father when he stopped by for a drink while sorting out the various bits of paper he always seemed to have about him.

One afternoon soon after Victoria was 17, father and daughter went into the canteen and Victoria caught the eye of a student. He was much taller than she, with a moustache—a student of law who introduced himself as Enrique Magriña. When she was 20, he and Victoria became engaged although they did not in fact marry for another five years.

'I suppose my parents expected that any young girl would have some suitors. But I don't think my father was really very anxious for me to have a fiancé. It was not that he disapproved of Enrique. He thought I should become engaged to a Prince—"to the Emperor of Siam", he said.'

Enrique himself did not play an instrument, read music or have any pretensions to sing. 'What Enrique did', says Victoria,' was to read poetry to me. I loved the poems of Juan Ramón Jimenez and Gustavo Bequer. He read their poetry to me. That was a very good way to make me fall in love with him. It seemed to me that the world was such a beautiful place. It was a long time before I could accept that it could be anything else but as beautiful as I saw it then.

'Enrique was quite entertaining and had a nice sense of humour. But he was not at all the romantic sort himself. He was not the kind of man to talk to you about the moon and that sort of thing. I was very shocked when I got to know him to discover that I was such a passionate person. I had to be very strong to contain and conceal my feelings. It would never have done for him to see how I felt. I could not be caught sighing in front of him!'

Pepe, the son that Bernardo was so proud to have, became the couple's chaperon. If they went to the cinema he went along with them. If they went for walks in the Ciutadella park, Pepe always came along too. 'We were watched very carefully,' Victoria remembers. 'Life was very strict for young people in those days. Today teenagers have their own discothèques to which we would never have been allowed to go. If it was the name day of a friend we went to their homes. But that was all that was officially allowed us. Sometimes if I just had to talk to Enrique alone I got away from the Conservatorio and met him in a café in the old part of the city. But I was terrified because my father seemed to know everybody in Barcelona. It was like living in a village.'

Enrique and Victoria slowly grew closer over the following eight years until it seemed inevitable that they should marry. The Spanish phrase for 'my wife'—'mi mujer'—literally means, 'my woman', and conveys all the proprietorial implications of marriage in Spain. If Victoria were to be Enrique's wife, then her talent, her career, her fame and her earnings were also to be his. He started to prepare to become Victoria's manager. He learned English and practised French. He bought a copy of Sol Hurok's *Impresario* and studied it at length. He discovered a suitable flat in the Calle Calvet, not far from the university.

It should not be thought that Victoria objected to having her affairs taken over so completely. On the contrary, it was only what she expected of her husband-to-be. 'He was marvellous,' she says. 'He looked after everything. He planned it all, designed and decorated the flat, and when I was carried over the threshold, there it was, all ready and waiting.'

Enrique's over-all design gave the house a comfortable, cool and traditional appearance. Curtains kept the glare of the sunlight out, and inside the lighting was discreet. A number

61

of silver standing and table lamps avoided any too dazzling light. The pictures on the walls came in gilt frames. There were a number of good still-life paintings of fruit and flowers among them.

Enrique's study was lined with good leather-bound editions and his gramophone was tucked away out of sight among the shelves. Victoria's grand piano had been brought down from the university, along with the screen that had given her a much-needed sense of privacy when she had practised in her studio in the caretaker's flat. The various rooms in her new home had marbled tile floors which helped to keep them cool and fresh—even on the most humid of Barcelona's summer days. In coming down in the world from the university heights she found her house—only some ten blocks away in the direction of Tibidabo—was much less exposed to the elements, much less liable to accumulate inside it the reflected heat of the summer.

At the back the couple had a plant-filled patio garden. The walls of the house had been slatted and creeper had been trained along the woodwork around suspended flower pots trailing greenery. Victoria loved to sit out among the plants on the wooden garden seat that Enrique had had placed in their shade. From there she could listen to the trilling of an exotic bird they kept in an elaborate, almost gothic cage suspended from a frame which stood on the floor looking like an upright magnifying glass in shape.

It was not long before the house was soon enlivened by the sound of dogs, the Irish Setters which Enrique now began to breed. The first was called Wotan after the Wanderer in *The Ring* cycle and the daughter he sired was also given a Wagnerian name, the enchantress Kundry from *Parsifal*. In dipping into Wagner to find names for their dogs they showed the same enthusiasm for mixing up source material as Wagner himself liked to exercise on the legends that he drew upon—or so at least Victoria felt.

On one of the beds upstairs Victoria kept her collection of dolls which had been growing steadily since her early teens. In the overseas tours which now soon followed, Enrique was to tell reporters anxious for some 'human background' that his wife had well over a hundred of them. Victoria's recollection is that the number was much smaller and that in the course of personal publicity it got greatly exaggerated. But wherever she went during the next few years she came home with a few more.

Meanwhile, Victoria fulfilled her first professional engagement in London. It came about by chance. Members of the *Ars Musicae* had been singing the praises of their protégée to friends in London. One of them had a contact at the B.B.C. After a little research, an enlightened producer asked that Victoria should sing Salud in *La vida breve* by Manuel de Falla.

'Strangely enough, I had never come across the opera before, but as soon as I read the score I realised that Salud was a character that I could identify with. She is so much in love, and is so utterly destroyed when she discovers that he is going to marry someone else. I found her conception of love to be very similar to my own. Although I never thought for a moment that Enrique really would run off with someone else, I only had to consider it to become Salud and to experience her pain. I had to learn the part in English, and of course I didn't speak a word of the language at the time, but after a month of studying it on my own in Barcelona, I thought that I was ready.'

At the beginning of March 1948, Victoria flew to London. This time she took two companions, her mother and the guitarist Renata Tarrago, daughter of Graciano Tarrago who had taught her the guitar at the Conservatorio. They stayed at a small hotel off Regent Street, and Victoria at once fell in love with London and with all things English. She remains a confirmed anglophile to this day.

The London that Victoria first saw was very different from that to which she is accustomed thirty years on. There were huge gaps in the streets, bomb craters and piles of rubble, sombre relics of five years of the Blitz. These, together with the rationing and the ubiquitous queues, reminded her of her own city recovering from war. The skyline then was still dominated by the well-known landmarks of Westminster Abbey, the Houses of Parliament, and Westminster Cathedral rather than the great high-rise office blocks which now dwarf them. Londoners understand it only when they are homesick, but to Victoria, as to so many foreigners, the town had a dour pride, a mysterious grandeur such as she has encountered nowhere else in the world.

'We even had one of the famous thick fogs on that first visit. There were red buses and red trams and the old-fashioned black taxis all creeping through the thick mists. It was colourful and mysterious, just like the London that we'd always read about.'

The B.B.C. was to be congratulated for years to come on their foresight in engaging Victoria so early in her international career. She gave two song recitals, accompanied by Renata Tarrago, and her first performance of *La vida breve* was greeted with rave reviews.

'They all said that it was a wonderful Salud, but I must confess that I didn't think that I had done anything special. When I came to perform it later on stage, I was glad that I had first sung it on the wireless. On stage, the dance segments are often more attractive to the audience than the singing.'

Both performances were broadcast live. The first went out on the Home Service on March 10. The second, with the B.B.C. Symphony orchestra conducted by Stanford Robinson, went out on the Third Programme on March 13.

Ernest Newman, music critic of *The Sunday Times,* returned home very tired on the night of the first performance. By chance, he switched on the wireless. His tiredness soon evaporated.

'I have been waiting thirty-five years, ever since *La vida breve* was published, to hear a performance of this little opera of Manuel de Falla of which the B.B.C. have given us two welcome broadcasts within the last two days (the orchestra score, by the way, differs from that of the piano). This is the kind of work in connection with which the B.B.C. can be of the greatest service to us; it is too short and dramatically too slight to be a practical proposition for the commercial theatre yet the music of it is much too good to be lost to the world.

'The ordinary music-lover knows nothing of the work except

64

the dance at the end of Act 2, Scene i, which is occasionally butchered to make a solo fiddler's exhibitionist holiday.

'The performances were very enjoyable, the orchestra playing with exceptional sensitiveness under Stanford Robinson and Flora Nielsen and Richard Lewis singing very well as the grandmother and Paco respectively.

'The Salud, Victoria de los Angeles, whom I cannot remember having heard before, is evidently a singer of unusual distinction; and she was the only one who knew how the "oriental" turns in Spanish melody should be sung. I listened to her in a recital of Spanish folk songs on Monday and was again struck by the beauty of her voice and the genuine musical quality of her singing.'

All the reviews stressed these qualities; her voice and her musicianship.

The head office of H.M.V. in London was also quick off the mark in signing Victoria to an exclusive contract. The head of the company's classical division, David Bicknell, was aware that the company's future depended upon those performers as yet unknown because of the exigencies of war, whose talents had been fostered during the six years of silence. He had been much impressed by the sample recording which Victoria had made in Spain, and wasted no time in snapping her up on her arrival in London. Artist and recording manager became respected friends. 'I would have been lost without his guidance', says Victoria. 'I was a complete newcomer and he seemed to know everyone and everything and had been with H.M.V. since the 'twenties. It was a great stroke of luck for me.'

At the famous Abbey Road studios, she made the first of the twenty-three recordings which she was to make there in the course of the next thirty years.

All in all, Victoria was kept so busy on her visit to London that she had the chance to use only two of the dozen letters of introduction that she had brought with her. The first was to the Spanish composer and pianist, José Iturbi, who was then in his early fifties and at the height of his popularity. He was one of the first and one of the most successful of the classical musicians who took their talents to Hollywood and played themselves and their instruments in films, thus affording a 'cultural' status to pulp romances and musicals. He had adopted, too, a decidedly Hollywood lifestyle. 'I was rather overawed by his very grand suite at the Hyde Park Hotel,' Victoria remembers. 'He had not one but *two* pianos. He was very charming and welcoming, but I think I must have seemed like a nervous schoolgirl fan.'

The most important letter that Victoria had brought with her in her voluminous handbag was from Anatole Fistoulari, with whom she had performed in Spain. It was addressed to David Webster, General Administrator, at the Royal Opera House, Covent Garden.

An invitation came to audition, and she sang arias from *Manon* and *La Bohème*, operas which, ironically, would soon be brought back into the Covent Garden repertoire specifically in order that she should make guest appearances there. On the occasion of this first audition, however, Victoria's performance was greeted by those fatal words, spoken gently for fear of causing hurt, 'Thank you very much. You will be hearing from us.'

No further word ever reached Victoria. When she made her Covent Garden debut in *La Bohème* in 1950, she did not remind David Webster of this audition. No one seemed to remember or, perhaps, cared to remember, that the *prima donna* had been rejected only two years before.

Back in Barcelona, Victoria was soon busy preparing an extensive recital tour of Spain. One of the engagements on the tour was to be a special family one in Barcelona. It signalled the breaking up of the secure López García ménage at the university, the bedrock of Victoria's achievements. Carmen was to be married in the university chapel. Victoria sang at the celebrations and was deeply moved. She thought to have a similar wedding in November.

José Maria Lamaña would not hear of it. She owed it to her friends and supporters to have a great public wedding. He fulfilled this, his last duty as her manager, with all the fastidiousness, enthusiasm and style which had characterised his every duty to date. The marriage was to be solemnised on November 20, 1948, at Iglesia de la Concepción in the smart Calle de Aragón. An orchestra and chorus were engaged to perform the wedding music, and the leading members of Barcelona society were invited. By now, Victoria was a popular and respected performer both in Barcelona and in Madrid. There would be many uninvited well-wishers, too, for Catalonia was proud of its daughter who had won glory in Geneva.

'I was quite sure of what I was doing', says Victoria, 'but it still worried me that I had to leave my parents. I knew that it had to happen sometime, but I was still very sad when it did.'

Victoria prepared carefully for the wedding. 'I designed the wedding dress myself. There were many people surrounding me who wanted to advise me how to dress, how to do my hair, what sort of make-up I should have. But I always had had my own ideas and had applied them over the years without saying too much.

'I think I had revolted some years before when I went with the *Patronato* to the Liceo. In the box in the interval, they had said, "Oh, Victoria, we don't like the way you have done your hair. Let's show you how it should be done." And they took all the pins out and stuck it back the way they thought it should have been done. That offended my pride a little. I started to take a much firmer line about the way I looked and I had always thought of designing my own wedding dress.

'I know that the people who had been anxious to give me advice had wanted me to look more elegant, more beautiful and had given their advice with the very best motives. I did take their opinions into account. But I had found my own dressmaker who made the wedding dress and my other dresses according to my desires which were always for very simple things.

'It was a wonderful period for fashion as well as for the arts and music after the war. After all the long years of austerity and hardship people were coming to life again. It was a hopeful time—not tired and cynical like today—and people were receptive to all sorts of ideas.'

Victoria arrived in a great black limousine to find huge crowds gathered about the church. Children were being carried shoulder high in order that they should catch a glimpse of the celebrated bride. When Victoria took her father's arm and entered the church, groups of cheering people closed in behind them. Bernardo López was in high spirits, but already looked a little hunched and frail as he walked up the aisle with his daughter. She wore an ivory satin dress of classic simplicity with a V-neck and tight-fitting sleeves buttoned at the wrists. She carried white carnations. Her only jewellery was a pair of simple pearl earrings.

Everyone who had thus far played an important part in Victoria's life was gathered under the high fluted arches of the church. She nodded, or gave a little smile of acknowledgment as she passed them—Dolores Frau, her *Ars Musicae* friends, the members of *El Patronato*, colleagues from the Conservatorio and the Liceo, students and graduates of the university, many of whom had graduated years before. The Orfeon Laudate sang the march from Handel's *Judas Maccabeus*. Smiling now, she took up her place at Enrique's side.

Afterwards, there was a grand reception at the Ritz. Victoria was happy to see all her old friends but, as is usual on such occasions, she was not sorry when she and Enrique could at last escape the throng. Enrique, who has always had a passion for fast cars, had borrowed a sporty two-seater for the occasion. He terrified his bride by pushing it to its limits on the short but breathtaking cliff-side road to Sitges. They checked into their hotel as dusk began to gather, and took a long, soothing stroll along the palm-lined beach. 'All the excitement of Barcelona seemed many days and many miles away. Even my singing seemed unimportant then. I was very, very happy.'

They returned a week later. They did not immediately move into the new Calle Calvet flat, but returned for a few days to Victoria's childhood home. Both Victoria and her parents had wanted a chance to celebrate the wedding in circumstances more intimate than those of the Ritz.

At last they moved into the flat which was to be their home for the next twenty years. A large parcel awaited them. It was addressed in the precise hand of José Maria Lamaña. It contained all the management records of Victoria's career to date. Lamaña bowed out, as he had done everything, gracefully.

8

A glance at the de los Angeles balance sheets for the last months of 1948 might give the impression that Victoria was enjoying a prolonged holiday before and after her wedding. In fact, except for the week's honeymoon at Sitges, she was fully occupied preparing for an exceptionally busy year ahead. 1948 was the year in which she would sing the role of Elsa in Wagner's *Lohengrin*, for the first time. She was also engaged to make three full recital tours—her usual Iberian tour, one in Scandinavia and one in South America. Enrique had his hands full in his first year as her manager.

He had acquired, however, some experienced assistance. Sol Hurok's European partner, Leonidas Leonidoff, travelled to Barcelona from Paris in order to hear Victoria. He was impressed. A couple of quick-fire, imperious telephone calls, and Victoria found herself committed to two additional concert tours. Julian Uceda, who had represented Victoria in her first year of professional touring, continued to serve her interests in Spain, while Ernesto Quesada was put in charge of South and Central American operations.

For all that Enrique had the aid of top professional entrepreneurs, his first year still proved to be a baptism by fire. The Liceo season had ended on a sad note. The management reluctantly agreed to an increase in Victoria's fees for *The Mastersingers* but said the singer would have to beg if she was ever to reappear at the Liceo. The Scandinavian tour was jinxed from the moment they took off for Oslo. The Liceo season had ended in the last days of February, and they set off immediately from a wintry Barcelona. It grew still colder as they flew northward, and the little two-engined airplane was buffeted this way and that by icy storm winds.

They were battered and weary when at last they arrived, but the ordeal had hardly started. No preparations had been made for the concerts, save that the two thousand-capacity hall had been booked for two nights. There had been no posters, no advance publicity in the newspapers. Of the few Norwegians who had heard of Victoria, still fewer were aware of her presence.

Enrique was quick to seek the aid of the Spanish embassy, but although they did their best to organise a few newspaper interviews, their influence was negligible. Enrique spoke no Norwegian and hardly any English, so could achieve little on his own account, and on the night of the first recital, he discovered to his horror that only twenty-seven of the two thousand seats had been sold. He fretted and smoked and paced at the front of the theatre, hoping for a miracle, but at last he decided that he must tell Victoria the truth.

'He was trying to calm me,' Victoria laughs, 'but in fact I was much the calmer. I just couldn't help seeing the funny side of it. I think I rather shocked poor Enrique when I burst out laughing!'

The tiny audience made up in enthusiasm for its lack of numbers. Luckily, the press was in attendance. Their plaudits were unanimous. She was even hailed as 'the new Kirsten Flagstad'. These notices were hurriedly copied and sent on in advance to the other venues on the tour in order to avoid any further embarrassment. Between them, press notices and word of mouth ensured that the second concert was well attended. The Magriñas left Oslo considerably more confident than when they had arrived.

The tour took them by boat and train to Stockholm and

Helsinki. 'By the time we reached the Finnish-Russian border, I was in another world,' says Victoria. 'The Scandinavian winter was so dark and magical, like the ancient fairytales of my childhood. But then, I was accustomed to the sunlight of Spain. I'm sure there is nothing romantic about it to the people who live there.' In a sense, this part of the tour served as an extension of their honeymoon. They were touring for a brief spell at a leisurely pace, and the pressures upon them were few.

'Usually I am not a morning person. I just don't like the mornings. I much prefer the afternoons and the evenings. But I loved getting up in those cold mornings in Scandinavia and sitting down to a huge breakfast. I was quite relaxed and happy in those days and had not yet begun to have the problem of insomnia that came to me in the 1950s and which made the mornings even more unbearable.'

It was a short-lived respite. Soon they were in Paris, once more surrounded by the hurly-burly of city life, once more subjected to the attentions of producers and journalists, agents and conductors. It was a brief but significant visit. Victoria was to give a recital at the Salle Gaveau and was to make her first appearance at the Paris Opera, singing the part of Marguerite in Gounod's *Faust*. Parisians were intrigued by the young Spaniard's mastery of the two forms, recitals and opera, which had hitherto been regarded as distinct disciplines.

Victoria herself was a little taken aback both by lack of proper rehearsal for *Faust* and by the conditions of the production. The sets dated from 1908. Faust's desk was covered in real dust. The flowers in Marguerite's garden were well past their first bloom. There was no full rehearsal, but only a run-through with a piano, as if they were preparing a studio broadcast rather than for a drama. Victoria was therefore compelled to rely on the moves that she had learned over the years in the Barcelona Liceo productions.

At first all went well. As Victoria sat at the spinning wheel, her voice seemed all the fresher by contrast with the aged props and backdrops. In Act II, however, Marguerite returns from church with a prayer-book in her hand and meets Faust for the first time. Stage directions at the Liceo here differed drastically from those at the Paris Opera, for just as Victoria expected her Faust to take her arm, she looked up to see the little tenor standing far off backstage. She had to hurry over to him, but was anxious, too, to retain the demure and modest aspect expected of Marguerite. The audience might lose some sympathy for a delicate and pious tragic heroine who strode cross-stage like a hockey player. In a bid to reconcile these conflicting concerns, she contrived to mince at high speed brushing past the scenery. The tenor's expression changed from one of astonished concern to one of alarm. The scenery, which had had no practice at this sort of thing for forty years or more, wobbled. If it collapsed, he would have to continue singing while clasping the arm of a lunatic soprano with a couple of hundredweight of painted plywood resting on both their heads. It was not a prospect which pleased. Fortunately, Victoria steadied herself, arrived at the tenor's side, and contrived to finish the scene with aplomb.

Unbeknownst to Victoria, the newly-appointed General Manager of the New York Metropolitan was sitting in the stalls appraising these antics. The notes that he took that night were to ordain the whole course of Victoria's career in opera.

A brief visit to Barcelona, then, and they were off again to London. After a recording session at Abbey Road, they were to embark at Southampton for Cuba and South America via New York. Again, Enrique's inexperience nearly proved disastrous. Only on arrival in London did he realise that they needed visas if they were to pass through the United States. They had no visas.

Victoria attempted to charm and then to browbeat the necessary documents from the embassy staff in London, but her name was still unknown to the Americans, and Spanish passport holders were regarded with suspicion in those days. Her next thought was to go to Paris, where Leonidas Leonidoff, European Manager of an American-based concern, could surely overrule the oppressive forces of bureaucracy. David

Bicknell would not hear of it. No such trivia would interrupt his recording session. He applied to the embassy for them. The Magriñas were representatives of H.M.V. All the power of the mighty company supported their application, and woe betide the Anglo-American music business should they encounter any hindrance. It was a close run thing, but it worked. The visas arrived just as Enrique was about to return the tickets. Thus began with difficulty the most difficult tour of Victoria's life.

The journey out was uneventful enough, save in that Enrique discovered that he was no sailor and spent the journey looking rather like an olive. No sooner had they set foot in New York, however, than the trouble began. They had arranged that their luggage be taken to Grand Central Station. There, they would board a train for Miami and then fly from Florida to Cuba. They arrived at Grand Central. Their luggage did not. Frantic calls were made to the New York offices of the shipping line, but they merely served to confuse further an already confused situation. 'If we had waited in New York, we would have missed the flight to Cuba, so we had no choice but to give up our clothes as lost and take the train to Miami with nothing more than the clothes we stood up in. We had hardly any money in those days, the luggage was not insured, and we had set off from London with one-way tickets, trusting that the tour would be sufficiently successful to pay the return fare.

'When we got to New York I have to admit I hated it at first,' Victoria remembers. 'I found it so immense and overpowering. I did not know then that I was going to live there and grow to love it.

'But the American people I first had dealings with I liked from the start. They were such nice people with perhaps something of an inferiority complex vis-à-vis Europe. They can be too readily awed by Europe and its traditions. They have so much to be proud of in themselves. I only began to realise what a rich country it was when we made our first train journey south. When you begin to tour America as I was to do by train, car and plane, it offers you such a rich panorama of forests and mountains. You cannot believe it. You get a false impression of America when you see New York first. I did at the beginning; like everybody else I saw New York and its skyscrapers as America without realising what wonderful places lie beyond it.'

One way or another, the United States did a poor public relations job on this, Victoria's first visit. As the Magriñas went through customs, Enrique's smart new overcoat vanished, and with it his wallet. They now had ten dollars between them. By the time they arrived in Havana, even this sum had been whittled down to one dollar and a few cents.

When two scruffy, weary travellers arrived at the Hotel President without luggage, they were not exactly greeted as befits visiting celebrities. The receptionist sniffed. The manager eyed them with circumspection. Enrique reassured them. He would ring Ernesto Quesada, the manager of their South American tour. He would sort everything out. The staff listened with knowing smiles as Enrique dialled the number, asked to speak to Quesada, and was informed that he was ill and could not be reached.

Victoria was persuaded to unwind over a solitary meal while Enrique, stopping to snatch a quick snack in a cheap bar, set off to find Quesada. Over the past few months, Enrique's friends had observed that he was smoking a great deal more than in the past. Now, the lighter came out of his pocket roughly once every three minutes.

Quesada at last obtained credit for the Magriñas at the hotel, but when Victoria went to her first rehearsal, she discovered yet another problem. The appointed accompanist might have been capable of picking out the national anthem on the parish church harmonium, but she was clearly unequal to Victoria's requirements. 'It would have been quite impossible to perform in those circumstances. It would have destroyed me.'

With characteristic stubbornness and integrity, she dug her heels in. Fortunately, the management did not know that their recalcitrant star had no money. They conceded. The Austrian pianist Paul Berl, who lived in New York, was flown in. The tour could continue. After the successful opening at the Auditorium Theatre in Havana, they went on to Puerto Rico, Venezuela, São Paolo and Rio de Janeiro, stopping off at Recife and other smaller towns to give very intimate concerts. At one, indeed, there was an even smaller audience than that of twenty-seven which had turned up in Oslo. 'I nearly invited the twelve people there to come up on the stage,' Victoria remembers. 'It was a lovely concert—pure music-making with friends.'

For all the critical success and popularity that she enjoyed, it was nonetheless clear that her modest fees would not cover expenses *and* buy return tickets for Enrique and herself. Enrique therefore approached the management of the Rio concert hall and sent a telegram to Quesada asking that there should be an extra benefit concert. This turned out to be much better organised than some of the previous concerts. The receipts saved the day. Victoria was then able to retrace her steps through South America, again giving concerts wherever she stopped, and so at last back to Spain.

They were both exhausted, nervously and physically, and took a long summer holiday on the Catalan coast. They did not know that this was the last uninterrupted holiday they would enjoy together for some 30 years.

9

Victoria finally made her La Scala debut on November 17, 1950, just a few days after her twenty-sixth birthday. Milan was the starting-point of her first Italian recital tour, which would also take in Rome and Florence. The Milanese are slow to accept the overblown claims of aliens, quick to acknowledge and welcome true quality. They gave their unqualified seal of approval to the young Spaniard. Antonio Ghiringhelli, the Superintendant of La Scala, and his colleague Luigi Oldani (who had made the abortive telephone call to Victoria in Geneva three years earlier), were crowing with delight at their coup. This was a triumph to be consolidated. At once they invited her to appear as Ariadne in Strauss's *Ariadne auf Naxos* which was to be performed on May 27 next year.

This was an important performance; even, in some ways, a premiere. Although *Ariadne* had first been heard in Vienna nearly forty years earlier, Strauss had revised the work in 1916. That this revision had not been performed in the world's major opera houses was due in part to the opera's origins. It was originally conceived as a brief *divertissement*, an interlude in Molière's farce, *Le Bourgeois Gentilhomme*. It had proved sufficiently popular for the composer to expand it into a full-length work. Molière's Paris was exchanged for a *nouveau riche* Viennese setting, but the new opera still demanded both opera singers and stage actors.

The revised version called for Victoria to play the part of Ariadne in the opera proper but not that of the *prima donna* in the prologue. As Ariadne, she had to spend a great deal of her time being morose and woeful to infect her with her *carpe diem* philosophy with joyous coloratura admonitions. Four comedians exhaust themselves in vain in a bid to make her laugh. She remains resolutely dejected. When at last she does find relief in the arms of the young god Bacchus, it is only for the rather devious reason that she mistakenly believes him to be the messenger of death. 'It is a fascinating role', says Victoria, 'and certainly a far cry from the Mimìs and Marguerites that I had been playing until then. It was my first and last Strauss opera role.'

She was to return to La Scala in 1951 to sing Donna Anna in *Don Giovanni*, in 1952 for Agatha in Weber's *Der Freischütz* and in 1956 for Rosina in *The Barber of Seville*. The first of these engagements was a direct consequence of her performance in *Ariadne auf Naxos*, for among the glittering audience at La Scala for the gala premiere was Herbert von Karajan. He approached her immediately after the performance. He was to direct and conduct a spectacular new production of *Don Giovanni* in January of the next year. Elisabeth Schwarzkopf was to play Elvira. Victoria had considerable reservations as to her suitability for so dramatic a role, but von Karajan was reassuring. He wanted a lyrical rather than a dramatic interpretation.

For all her misgivings, Victoria looked forward to working with the maestro and with Schwarzkopf, her brilliant contemporary, whose natural talents and dedicated musicianship she much admired. She learned the role, as always, unaided, in the following months.

Contention first arose because of the date on which Victoria was due to arrive in Milan. January 6 is, of course, Epiphany, and an important religious festival in Spain. Victoria therefore asked that she be permitted to arrive on the following day. The Catholic Italians understood and readily granted permission, but Karajan was displeased.

Further problems arose when Victoria arrived in Milan.

'When will I be called for the first piano rehearsal?' she asked eagerly.

'The maestro never has them,' came the blunt reply.

'Then what *does* the maestro have?'

'Stage rehearsals.'

Karajan at that time was a very enthusiastic stage director of works he conducted and was himself producing *Don Giovanni*. So, after many days' stage rehearsals, he said '*Proviamo alla Italiana*', which meant that musical rehearsal was to be a simple line-up in front of full orchestral rehearsal.

Victoria attended the first rehearsal and, as is her usual practice, did not sing out. Von Karajan stopped the rehearsal at once with one of those studied, beautiful, imperious gestures which have relegated composers to second billing on record sleeves and concert posters.

'Madame,' he said, 'you are not singing full out. You must use all your voice.'

Victoria felt like asking, 'Why?' but contented herself with posing the more immediate problem. 'But Maestro', she said, 'I am only just feeling my way into the part. You and I, after all, have had no musical rehearsal together. If, as a result, countless hours must be wasted while we get it right, you cannot blame me.'

A hard edge entered von Karajan's voice. 'You will sing full out as I tell!' he spat.

The rehearsal was resumed, but now Victoria did not sing at all. She went through the moves and opened her mouth at suitable points, but no sound emerged from her lips. Von Karajan, visibly shocked, sang the role of Donna Anna himself. No words were exchanged at the end of the rehearsal. Von Karajan strode off in one direction; Victoria shrugged and went her own way. Soon, however, as anticipated, von Karajan's complaints reached her via the management. She was undisciplined and wilful. She would not obey her conductor. He, von Karajan, would not be gainsaid.

Eventually some high-powered diplomacy appeased these two strong spirits and the production settled down. But it would be a mistake to see this episode as a great rift between international stars. Although by coincidence Victoria never sang under von Karajan's baton again, neither she nor the conductor have regarded the argument as anything more than one of the innumerable differences of opinion inevitable in any artistic production.

While in Rome that season, Enrique was approached by a journalist anxious to make the most of Victoria's growing international celebrity.

'You have heard, of course,' said the eager hack, 'that there is another very successful singer, one Maria Callas, who is creating something of a sensation in Italy at the moment?'

'Of course I have heard about Callas,' said Enrique. 'She is said to be a remarkable performer.'

'Well, do you think that you could arrange for your wife to say, or better still, to write a few things attacking Callas? A letter or two, you know, just saying that Callas is a charlatan, things like that. You could write them for her, or I could, if you'd like. . . .'

Enrique was bemused. 'But why on earth should we attack Callas? I really don't understand. I have heard that she is anything but a charlatan, that she is a magnificent singer. . . .'

'Ah, yes, Mr Magriña, that's as may be, but, you see, we would publish the letters on the front page. Then we could arrange for your wife to dine in the same restaurant as Callas and we could arrange a fight, and then . . .'

Enrique allowed him to continue no further. 'But I did not know whether to laugh or cry when I heard about it,' says Victoria. 'Nothing is easier than to get that sort of publicity and there is nothing that I would sooner not have.'

But publicity now attended Victoria's every move unbidden. Whatever the word 'star' may mean, Victoria was now acknowledged throughout the world to be just that. 'It had just happened naturally,' she now recalls wistfully. 'I still didn't regard what I was doing as very special. I would have been quite happy to have given it all up to stay at home and have a family.'

To be a Spanish artist in London at the end of the 1940s and the beginnings of the 1950s had a dimension of exoticism to it that is not easy to appreciate from the vantage point of the 1980s. The war in Spain and World War II meant that Spain was a country comparatively few people had visited. Its borders were only just being reopened at the time of Victoria's visits and trading links were only just beginning to be established. The English were certainly fascinated by Spain. But very few dared to holiday in a country where trains and roads were reputed to be very poor indeed. In July 1951 Franco was to dismiss most of his cabinet with the avowed object of strengthening the country's relations with the Western World, America in particular. It was the first move that would eventually bring mass tourism to Spain and send many Spanish people to work in the rest of Europe. But at the beginning of the 1950s Spain still remained fascinatingly remote and the Englishman's fascination at this time was able to find an outlet in the repertoire of Spanish songs that Victoria brought with her in her recital tours of Britain. They inspired the same sort of enthusiasm that awaited Spanish dancers in the United Kingdom at this time like Teresa and Luisillo, Rosario and Antonio, and José Greco.

For her single appearance at Covent Garden as Mimì in *La Bohème* on March 1, 1950, Victoria made her debut singing in Italian as the home team came back at her in English. Despite this extraordinary arrangement, the evening was a success. The B.B.C. *Vida breve* performances of 1948, and the gramophone recordings that had been issued afterwards had ensured a packed and expectant house. The following morning, March 2, *The Times* made it clear just how important the evening had been. The paper's critic wrote:

> In the true manner of a Puccini heroine, Miss Victoria de los Angeles introduced herself to the country first as a voice, a voice on gramophone records before appearing in person last night. However she arrived at Covent Garden for what is to be her only appearance as Mimì this season.
>
> It is rare to discover such maturity of tone in one so young. This was apparent from the very start, though in

the first act nervousness played havoc with her production. But, after acclimatising herself to her surroundings throughout the comparative respite of the second act she was in complete control of the third where it soon became evident that she was a singer of the front rank with plentiful reserves of tone as well as tenderness, and phrasing that was a delight in its effortless shapeliness. A natural sturdy appearance made it the harder for her to suggest the physical leanness with which Puccini here accompanies the emotional frailty of one of his typical little women. In fact Mimì's fate moves us less than Miss de los Angeles's voice. The orchestral playing under Mr Warwick Braithwaite had its moments . . .

In *The Sunday Times* Ernest Newman did not fail to remind his readers that he had already signalled the arrival of a great artist at the time of her arrival in 1948. He wrote:

A year or two ago Victoria de los Angeles was quite unknown in this country, but she made a great impression on a few people who listened to her in the B.B.C.'s broadcast of Falla's opera *La vida breve*; and since then she has made three or four gramophone records that have attracted attention. On Wednesday evening, at Covent Garden, we heard the young Spanish singer for the first time in the flesh, as Mimì in *La Bohème*.

She fully confirmed our first impression of her as an artist quite out of the common. The possessor of a beautiful voice, powerful and delicate by turns, a mistress of all the arts of tonal shading, one who has not merely studied singing but is a singer born and, to top it all, a musician who can satisfy the critical listener's most exigent demands in the matter of style, phrasing and so on. We shall all be interested to hear her again in an opera of another type.

Two days later, on Saturday, March 2, with Gerald Moore as her accompanist for the first time, she made her recital debut at the Wigmore Hall. Once again *The Times* left its readers in no doubt of the importance of the occasion when its critic wrote the following Monday morning:

Miss Victoria de los Angeles is a great artist; her recital in Wigmore Hall on Saturday evening left no doubt of that. Gramophone records and an appearance at Covent Garden had made us aware of her expressive, powerful voice, capable of assuming a warmer *mezzo* quality on occasion, but it was left to this recital to reveal her fine musicianship. She moved with assurance and certainty of style from early Italian opera via Handel— the coloratura passages in "O, had I Jubal's lyre" were executed with agile lucidity—to the German romantic *Lied*, whose spirit is as far removed as possible from her native Spain. Yet Miss de los Angeles conveys this introspective element with pronounced success, just as though the Prater and the Generalife were next door neighbours and equally dear to her heart. If she did not quite suggest the co-existence of words and tone that Brahms and Schumann achieved, it was largely because in foreign languages, she has not yet conquered the Spanish habit of softening those consonants which in German song are all-important. But, however impeccable her manners, however convincing her vocal disguise, in foreign territory, there could be no doubt that Falla and his compatriots display this wonderful voice to best, because most natural, advantage; in the Spanish group that ended the recital she gave us the whole voice and the whole artist with results that will not soon be forgotten.

'After the London recitals, we travelled to Scotland for the Edinburgh festival,' Victoria remembers. 'It was a marvellous experience and the best part of it was hearing, and meeting, Kathleen Ferrier for the first time. What a beautiful voice she had, and what an exceptional artist she was. The audiences loved her for her simplicity, her honesty in all things musical and the humanity of her voice, which I remember Maestro Bruno Walter saying was unique.

'She was giving a recital with Bruno Walter at the piano.

I knew that she was in Edinburgh but had no idea where she was staying. I was being put up in the house of some friends who had a lovely music room where I could prepare my recital on the piano. One morning I was preparing my programme singing at the piano when the door opened and a woman came in I had never met before. She was wearing a dressing-gown and looked very attractive although she was wearing no make-up and her hair was still damp. She said, "I knew that could only be the voice of Victoria de los Angeles. Hello, I'm Kathleen Ferrier." I was very moved by her simple directness—it was a quality everybody seemed to love in her.

'A few years later, in 1953, we knew she had become seriously ill and that there was no hope of her getting better. In February, Gluck's *Orfeo* had been staged for her at Covent Garden, but she had only been well enough to give two performances. Enrique and I were passing through London at the beginning of October and, between trains, we sent some flowers to the hospital where they were nursing her. We had a terrible shock a few days later in South Africa. The concierge of the hotel where we were staying delivered a letter and a newspaper to Enrique at the same time. In the newspaper there was a photograph of her with the news that she had died. The letter was from Kathleen, to thank us for the flowers. Her death was a terrible blow, not only to the world of music but to everyone who had known her.'

10

Backstage at Carnegie Hall immediately before a concert is not the most pacific of places at the best of times. On October 24, 1950, the night on which Victoria de los Angeles was billed to make her U.S. concert debut, it was bedlam. Backstage dramas are, of course, as common, and frequently more intense, than those on stage. The only difference, indeed, between this one and a Victorian melodrama was that no one could hear a word that anyone was saying.

The only silent character was the languishing heroine. The remainder of the distinguished cast, comprising doctors, musicians, hard-hearted businessmen and distraught husband, all declaimed mightily.

Victoria had contracted sinusitis.

It had started with a heavy cold picked up on the Atlantic crossing. She had thought that the worst was over when she arrived to an enthusiastic reception from the American press and public, but the discomfort had increased. Matters were not helped by the no-expenses-spared publicity campaign which Sol Hurok had launched weeks before her arrival. Every radio listener in New York had heard Victoria's performance of *La Maja y el ruiseñor* as regularly as the advertisements for breakfast cereals. The city's most distinguished musicians and critics, of course, had already heard of the stir which Victoria had caused in Europe. They would all be there to see what the fuss was about.

The management declared that they would hold out to the last. They were confident that the renowned throat specialist whom they had called in would alleviate the symptoms of the illness at least for a couple of hours.

The management was adamant. With a full house of New York's finest expected, they just could not call off the concert. The doctor equivocated. He had had some success, he said. It would not harm Victoria to go on stage, but she could count on no more than seventy per cent of her voice. The decision, then, was Victoria's. Wisely and, perhaps, disingenuously, she passed it on to Hurok. He did not hesitate. Too much was at risk. She would not make her American debut under par. He simply scribbled, 'Regret recital cancelled due to indisposition.' The management woefully posted the text on the doors shortly before the public began to arrive.

Nine days later, it was decided to try again. By this time, Victoria was said to be ninety per cent recovered. For the rest, she could count on her experience and artistry to see her through. Again the public turned up in force, headed by such as Marian Anderson, Arturo Rubinstein, Isaac Stern and many other distinguished performers. It was easily the most critical audience to whom Victoria had performed.

If there were any doubts that the public might have been upset by the last-minute cancellation of the first recital, they were quickly dispelled. Accustomed to the cool, often remote authority of so many New York concerts, the audience was won over both by Victoria's singing and by the no-nonsense style in which, at the end of the evening, she drew out her guitar and performed a large selection from her Spanish repertoire. There was encore after encore. A few hours later, the critics confirmed and consolidated the young soprano's triumph. The critic of *The New York Herald Tribune* rhapsodised about this 'golden voice'.

The New York Times reviewer, Olin Davis, was more guarded:

(*Above*) Victoria as Salud in Falla's
La Vida Breve, a role which helped
to launch her international career

(*Right*) Victoria as Marguerite in
Faust, her debut role at the Paris
Opera and at the Metropolitan, with
Jussi Björling

(*Above*) As Rosina in *The Barber of Seville* at La Scala

(*Opposite*)
Singing Agatha in *Der Freischütz* at La Scala during her year's leave of absence from the Met in the mid-1950s

(*Left*) Victoria sings the title-role of *Ariadne auf Naxos* in her debut at La Scala where Strauss' opera was given for the first time in May 1950

(*Top*) As Desdemona, with Mario del Monaco in the title role of *Otello*, (*above*) as Eva in *Die Meistersinger*, and (*right*) as Mélisande, one of Victoria's most cherished roles at the Met

The Tyrone Guthrie revival of *La Traviata* at the Metropolitan in the late 1950s

(*Above*) Manon, a role—like Butterfly and Mimì—which will always be associated with Victoria

(*Opposite top*) On the swing in the Met's lavish revival of Flotow's *Martha*, Victoria's least favourite role and her last for the Met

(*Opposite bottom*) Rehearsing *Tannhäuser* with Wieland Wagner at Bayreuth in the 1960s

(*Left*) Victoria in Zeffirelli's *verismo* production of *Pagliacci* at Covent Garden

As Carmen, the role Victoria always wanted to sing in her early years at the Met

Victoria de los Angeles, the Spanish soprano, had been loudly heralded in advance of her recital last night in Carnegie Hall. The hall was packed. Enthusiasm ran high throughout the evening. Whatever Miss de los Angeles did was vigorously applauded, and she could have repeated more songs than one by Falla of her last group. At the end of her recital she sat at the piano and accompanied some Spanish encores on the guitar.

But now the tumult is over, it is to be said that Miss de los Angeles gave a series of singularly uneven performances. She has a fine authority of manner, poise, various effective devices of interpretation and a voice of much natural beauty, variously produced. The middle part of it is finest in quality, control and tone, flexibility and skilful coloring for interpretative purposes, and everything is expressive.

The beginning was highly authoritative; the noble recitative aria from the virtually unknown opera *Orpheus* by Monteverdi. This was vocal declamation of the most dignified sort, whether the visitor knew a word of the text or not. A familiar song of Scarlatti was sung neatly, lithely and archly—a little too archly. The triumph of this group and a high-water mark of the recital was the air about Jubal's lyre from Handel. Its long, florid phrases were tossed off with virtuosity, breath control and coloratura stylishness and brought down the house. Here the business of enunciation was negligible. The essence of the aria is of course its exuberant ornamentation, and here Miss de los Angeles showed one of her principal assets.

Sol Hurok's prudence was well-rewarded. On the tide of the success of this debut, he booked two additional concerts. Both were immediately sold out.

One unexpected bonus for Victoria was to meet the great violinist, Isaac Stern. Over the years this vital and exuberant man was to become a close friend. His first reaction to her voice, however, is indicative of the enthusiasm Victoria's singing prompted in almost everyone who heard her during these years. Victoria remembers with gratitude his praise after a concert she gave in Boston a few years later. 'He lived there, you know, and I had gone there for a concert with the Symphony Orchestra. I sang *Nuits d'été* with the Boston Symphony Orchestra and recorded it a few days later with them. Charles Munch was conducting. Anyhow, after the concert, Stern came round to see me and announced, "I was very moved by the sound of your voice."' Stern has always remained a great admirer of her art.

'A few days later, he insisted on coming along to the recording sessions that we were doing. He sat there, totally impassive. Then, at the end, he said to me, "I wanted to get used to the sound of your voice so that I can look for it in my violin."'

The Carnegie Hall recitals and the acclaim came before Victoria's operatic debut at the Metropolitan, which was not to occur until March of the following year. This was in keeping with the de los Angeles convention. Ever since her debut in Barcelona in 1944, Victoria always prefaced a first appearance in a new opera house with a recital in the same city.

'I never wanted to be known as an opera singer who also gave recitals,' she explains. 'On the contrary, I hoped to be accepted as a recitalist who also sang operas. The recital world is of course a minority world, but oh, what a wonderful minority! A marvellous public attends recitals, though I find that they are very cautious about going to the opera. I think that a singer who made her name in opera and then tried to establish herself as a recitalist would find it very difficult. The recital world would probably say, "She's an opera singer. Not quite right for us." I always wanted very much to be accepted as a recitalist, so I gave a recital first and then, if the public liked me and my music, they could come and hear me in opera, too.

'I find the recital world more fruitful, more natural and altogether more logical than opera. In the opera house there are so many things competing with the music—the make-up, the costumes, the lighting, the stage-director, the conductor. You, the singer, are constantly aware of so many conflicting things as you try to put across the music that it is an immense joy to be able to leave all that behind and to put across your own personality, your own brand of music.'

This policy has served Victoria well. In the 1950s, when much of her time was spent in the opera house, she found relief from the strain imposed by endless gala nights in her separate recital career. After the mid-1960s, too, when family responsibilities prevented her from committing herself to long winter seasons of opera, her recital tours gave her independence and a very much more flexible timetable. And then, as the years have taken their toll and regular operatic appearances have grown more taxing, Victoria has been able to continue her performing career in the recital halls when many another singer must long since have retired.

'On the recital platform, it is your personality which is on show. That is the point of it and the joy of it. So, when I make up a recital programme, I choose what I hope will reflect my personality at the given time. Generally, I divide the programme into four parts. The first, which is usually made up of ancient music, is there to establish the colour of my voice. Then I have a section of German *Lieder*. The third section is of French or Italian music, or a mixture of the two, and I finish with my Spanish songs.'

Her repertoire is extraordinarily wide. The records show that she has drawn on fifty different programmes incorporating well nigh a thousand songs.

'All thanks to *Ars Musicae*, of course. When first I sang with them, there was the possibility that I might have to sing *zarzuelas*, musicals and that sort of light music. Then the other members of the group asked me why I didn't branch out into *Lieder*. I studied Schubert and Schumann with them and, at the same time, began to learn some of the ancient music of Spain whose performance had been, until my arrival, the group's *raison d'être*. One way and another, in the course of music-making, I was introduced to an enormous range of composers. It all happened quite naturally and spontaneously. I never made a conscious effort to be "different" or erudite. It was just that we all enjoyed every kind of music. The result was that when I came to do my first recitals, it seemed quite natural to make up my programmes from all those sources.

'I have often been asked why, being Spanish and a lyrical soprano, I sing *Lieder*. It's meant to be a totally different style of singing, you know. Well, obviously I have always tried to choose the more romantic, non-intellectual sort of *Lied,* the well-known songs by Schumann and Schubert. I love them, and would sing them anyhow for sheer pleasure, whether people wanted to pay to hear me do so or not. But even so, I do feel a little uneasy in this section. It is so hard to be accepted, and people have very fixed ideas as to how *Lieder* should sound. There is so much tradition surrounding the songs. I'm afraid that I don't believe in that sacred tradition. I remember that Lotte Lehmann used to say the same thing. She was very independent-minded and, of course, German, so she could say such things and get away with it. If you are Spanish and say them, you are held to be guilty of a terrible blasphemy.'

Despite the responsibility and the loneliness of the recitalist, who has not even a stage-director or a conductor to shape the performance, Victoria has never missed the guiding hand of a teacher. Most singers keep taking lessons all their lives, but she is adamant that a teacher is superfluous and even dangerous.

'I really do prefer to be left alone to sort things out for myself. The voice is the voice of the singer, not that of the teacher. Only the singer can know what is going on inside himself. I think that a singer must know himself inside out, both mentally and physically. He shouldn't have to rely on a teacher to tell him what is right or wrong. In working on my own, I have come to know my voice and to understand it in relation to the rest of me. I have never wanted to force it beyond its capabilities. A teacher often wants to control, even to change a voice. Sometimes they actually manage to destroy a voice.

'Oh, yes, sometimes I have wished that I had a little expert guidance. The voice changes over the years, and you have to adapt with it. Sometimes things go a little wrong. But I always devise medicines and disciplines for myself. By yourself, you very quickly realise when you are developing certain faults, then you examine your repertoire and maybe you have to decide to stop singing certain things. Perhaps a very good friend, or a conductor, may notice that you are developing this or that mannerism. Someone like that can open your eyes and then you have to analyse the problem, go off by yourself and sing and sing until you have sorted it out.

'I exercise a lot, but never at fixed hours. I find it impossible to say that I will do so many hours' work from this time to that every day. I just work in the most natural way. Some days, I even do absolutely no work from dawn till dusk. Perhaps I'm tired and unwell and it just will not come. But sometimes, when I feel fit and happy and able to think clearly, I will work for hours and hours.

'Then, of course, a lot of time is spent in preparing programmes. It can take ages to decide just what to sing at a particular concert. You cannot think of the songs in isolation. Each must be considered in relation to others and in relation to your own voice. You have to be sure that they fit together harmoniously both in terms of tone and in terms of meaning. You have to be sure how you will feel as you pass from one song to another.

'Apart from these basic considerations, though, I think that it is very dangerous to over-intellectualize. When I was younger, I never used to analyse even to this point because I wanted it all to happen spontaneously. Of course, a professional cannot afford such a hit or miss attitude, however good the hits may be, but I don't feel free and happy if I have the impression of being weighed down with too much conscious preparation, and if you are going to entertain people, you *must* feel free and happy. I always had a very romantic concept of music. For me, it was something that came from the soul, something not contrived but spontaneous—lifting you, fulfilling you naturally. Maybe it was not true—but I wanted to believe it. That's why it was very important for me to "discover" the songs on a programme for myself and by myself. The personality of each piece is so personal and so wonderful that I could not bear to have a *répétiteur*-type teacher hammering out the rhythm, "Tap-tap-tap . . . Again, Victoria. Sing it again. Tat-tap-tap-tap . . . Again! Like this . . ." That sort of thing would destroy all the wonder of music-making for me.

'It would be ridiculous for me to claim that I never make mistakes as a result of this approach. It is one thing to choose a song in your own studio at home, and it's quite another to find yourself in another country before an audience. Each nation, each town, each audience has a different effect on you. Sometimes I have gone out onto the platform and thought, "Oh, *why* did I ever choose that song for this place? It doesn't belong here at all!" And sometimes, too, I have found a song which I think will suit my voice, and then when I actually sing it, I think that I must have been out of my mind. But, of course, you have to give yourself challenges, you have to keep trying to sing risky, difficult pieces. You keep growing that way. But at the last, it's no good unless the public likes them. That is why over the years you find yourself repeating songs. You know what you communicate best.'

Sometimes members of Victoria's audience have been responsible for her choice of a song. Once, Balanchine asked her if she would consider performing Faure's *'Clair de Lune'*. 'I want to hear you sing it', he said, 'because I have often wanted to choreograph it. I think your voice might show me how.' She was flattered, but consigned the suggestion to the back of her mind. Only some months later did she come across the score in her studio, remember Balanchine's words and try the song for size. It was a great success.

Another person very closely involved with the presentation of a programme is, of course, the accompanist. The greatest of these, and one of Victoria's closest collaborators, Gerald Moore, remembers how Victoria's insistence upon spontaneity astonished others in the concert world. 'Sometimes I was completely in the dark about the programme we were to present until late in the day.'

When they toured together, so far from devoting weeks to

preparation as many audiences supposed, they merely met for a brief run-through before the recital began. Enrique would be in attendance on these occasions, preparing the lighting, for Victoria was very concerned always that the auditorium should not be too brightly lit so that her concentration would not be impaired.

'An accompanist must be a remarkable person with a rare, rare combination of gifts. He needs to be an artist, but also he must understand the creativity of the singer. He has to be adaptable in order to come to terms with the personality of each singer that he accompanies. These are very hard things to find. As if it weren't enough to seek a first-rate artist with that sort of modesty and adaptability, you cannot have a shrinking violet for an accompanist. He must have a streak of theatricality and flamboyance in his make-up. He, after all, is the presenter. He must not do anything which will interfere with the effect of the music, but at the same time he must create the sort of excitement and enthusiasm which turns a recital into a piece of theatre. Above all, the great accompanist must maintain that enthusiasm, his own creativity and his concentration, right up to the last minute. You must never lose that *ambience*.

'Of all the fine accompanists with whom I have worked, Gerald Moore was the greatest. He was unique. He always had the imagination to create something out of nothing while retaining total sympathy with the singer. He never let me—or himself—down.

'If ever I was low, physically or vocally, he had the power to lift me and carry me forward. He had what I would call mind-power. It never failed. You could begin a concert with him feeling absolutely dreadful, but he would never cut back on the accompaniment and start "playing down". Some accompanists get so upset if you are off form at the beginning that they play less and less with the result that you sing less and less. In the end, you both practically disappear under the piano. With Gerald it was exactly the opposite. He built you up when you were down. He willed you on, and you could feel it and hear it in his playing.

'It is marvellous to travel hundreds of miles and to find a musician of Gerald's calibre waiting for you in the concert hall, but oh, it is terrible to have prepared a programme at home, flown half-way across the world, and find some accompanist who is going to be the terror of your life behind the piano. In America once I was given a woman pianist, who, I discovered, just could not keep time. An accompanist like that can destroy you. You can be in wonderful voice. You can feel your imagination tingling bright and clear. Then little by little, the accompanist robs you of everything. Your spirits sag. Your voice begins to reflect your anxiety. Your concentration and imagination go. With Gerald, I always knew that all would be well and that I could rely on him. I could concentrate on deriving the most from each song. I can only thank God that he, and one or two other fine accompanists, were around during my career.

'For me, giving a recital is like going to a party. When you arrive at a party you know almost at once what sort of atmosphere there is going to be. You circulate for a while, talk to people, sound them out and rapidly get an idea what sort of evening you are likely to have. When you begin a recital, you listen for first reactions, and you quickly sense the sort of friends that you've got out there. I need to establish a close relationship with them. In 1980, for example, I gave a concert at the Wigmore Hall, and I was feeling very nervous because I had been rather ill and had had to make a cancellation. So I said, just to overcome my nervousness, "You may applaud if you wish"—and they did. Instantly we all relaxed. So, like a good party, a good recital is an opportunity to meet some nice people, relax in their company, and then you all go your own ways with memories of a happy time together.'

11

Viennese-born Rudolf Bing, newly-appointed General Manager of New York's Metropolitan Opera House, was on a shopping spree. Drawing on the extensive connections which he had established as a director of Glyndebourne and of the Edinburgh festival, he had come to Europe looking for new talent in accordance with his innovative policy. He caught Victoria at a recital in Paris, and immediately engaged her for the following season at 'The Grand Old Lady of Thirty-Ninth Street'.

Victoria's first performance at the Met was to be in *Faust* on March 17, 1951. The theatre had opened with a performance of *Faust* in 1883, and Gounod's opera had been revived so often since that the place had been nicknamed 'The Faustspielhaus'.

Before arriving in New York, Victoria had very little to do with Bing as the arrangements had been handled by Enrique. But once there she was immediately aware how it was made clear to everybody that this was now Mr Bing's Met. He was running the show and his forceful style of management differed from his more easy-going and popular predecessor, Edward Johnson. Nicknamed the 'Austrian Rodolfo', Bing's restless energy certainly kept him lean and hungry-looking and his alert moving eyes seemed to observe all that was going on and indeed some things that were not. Everything was referred to him and 'Mr Bing' was a name that was on everybody's lips though not always with the utmost amiability. The explanation seemed to lie in a saying of David Webster's, whose management style at Covent Garden was so different that it earned him the title of 'Quiet Showman'—in Montagu Haltrecht's biography. Webster remarked that 'an artist has a right to be temperamental but a temperamental manager is always wrong.'

'Hard-working' rather than temperamental would have been a fairer description of the Mr Bing Victoria encountered at the start of her years with the Met. His high, domed and balding head peered round the dressing-room doors before the curtain went up and could be seen shortly afterwards during the performance from his box where he did his entertaining of the wealthy and the powerful in public with the limelight fully on him. Victoria, who at this stage was as withdrawn as in her first days at school, kept well away from the managerial whirlwind.

The Met season had begun on November 6 and was drawing to a close when Victoria arrived. Bing's thoughts were already turning to the company's annual Spring tour of the nation. He was hoping that the arrival of a new star would help to maintain the lively momentum of his first year which had opened with immensely successful English-language productions of *Don Carlos* and *Die Fledermaus*. His hopes were well-founded. Victoria's first performances—first as Marguerite, then as Mimì and Madam Butterfly—so obviously proclaimed that another truly great soprano had joined the extraordinary roll of honour of the Met that excitement ran very high.

It may not have been a particularly happy time to arrive in the United States—McCarthyism was rampant, and McCarthy's witch-hunters had not ignored the world of music—but it was a fascinating time for those at the Met. Bing had applied a vigorous new broom, insisting on standards of professionalism which had declined gravely in the years immediately before. 'When I first arrived,' recalls Victoria, 'it was not yet quite time for new productions all round, new broom or no. At first, for example, we were still allowed to bring our own set of opera costumes.' Bing confessed that he blushed deeply for the sheer antiquity of the *Faust* production. It was only one of a whole series of 'condemned' productions which he would replace in the course of the next few seasons.

The reforms were long overdue. The Met had acquired the reputation of a museum as much as that of an opera house. All the latest developments in lighting, set-building and stagecraft on Broadway had been disregarded by successive managers. The orchestra was still held in high esteem, but singers appeared to be engaged on a totally haphazard basis. One seasoned observer wrote that, in those sure-fire successes, the universally popular French and Italian works, casts changed from performance to performance according to who just happened to be in town at the time. Bing changed all that. He engaged Victoria, as he engaged all his artists, for an unbroken span of ten to twelve weeks so that there should be long, disciplined rehearsals and a sense of continuity in the productions. He quickly displayed a keen eye for talent, and engaged such people from the theatre as Peter Brook, Alfred Lunt and Tyrone Guthrie to create the new productions. Not all of the operas, however, could be restaged immediately. *Faust* was one such casualty.

Victoria's greatest success with her new public was, perhaps predictably, in *Butterfly*. 'I felt so very close to Butterfly. It gave me much, much more than the enjoyment of singing. I had this wonderful, sustaining feeling of a rôle through which I could actually project *myself*. It is one of the longest vocal parts for a soprano, but that was never a problem because it so exactly suited my voice. I never had to think about technique when I was singing it. I never thought, "Now this note is coming" or "Now I have to do so and so." I could just give myself totally to the role. I felt that I *was* Butterfly.'

There had been, however, some directorial misgivings during the preparations for the first night of *Butterfly*. This was the only opera which Victoria had not sung previously. Bing suggested that Victoria should first perform in Bordeaux. Victoria asked him why. He shrugged and explained that these were to be dress rehearsals, as it were, for the gala opening. She did not like the idea, and did not respect his cautiousness. 'I always knew what I could do and what I could not. In that, I trusted my own judgment absolutely. I didn't see why we should do these trial runs, and told him so. When we arrived in Bordeaux, as always, I did not sing out during rehearsals, so the first time that I actually sang the part was on the first night in France.'

*   *   *

The Met critics were enthusiastic. One wrote: 'even the critics themselves were clapping', while several observed that Victoria's performance did not seem to be a stage characterisation. It all seemed too real, too natural, so great was the 'suspension of disbelief' engendered by Victoria's committed rendering of the part. She was Butterfly incarnate.

'They talked about great acting, but I'm not so sure. As I said, I never had to think how to sing the part, but when it was over, I felt a tremendous sensation of fulfilment and relief. Of course, the ideal thing is to be a very good actor *and* a very good singer, but, although I had the voice, I hadn't really the experience to be a really great actress. I just got into the character and stayed in the character. I believe very much in acting by instinct. Of course, technique plays a part, but all the technique in the world won't help you if you can't put something of yourself, something that you can feel sincerely, into your performance.'

At the end of the season, Bing signed Victoria for a second. She was now one of the Met's 'resident artists'. For all Bing's efforts to modernise and streamline the productions there, the opera house itself retained a unique character. It was delightfully primitive. You expected to see Lon Chaney skulking in the gallery and hear the distant strains of subterranean

100

organ music. There was no revolve, no rear or side stage, and the dressing-rooms were the sparsest that Victoria had ever known. But none of this worried her; indeed, she soon came to love the peculiar features of the house. As is so often the case, the uncomfortable conditions provided an eccentric atmosphere that would be remembered with affection.

The Met had, too, its long-standing traditions. On Tuesdays, for example, the theatre was always closed, and the whole troupe moved to Philadelphia. On Saturday afternoons sponsored broadcasts were given. This, a convention dating from the 'thirties, was intended to bring opera to a far wider audience than the house's own three-and-a-half thousand nightly visitors. 'This, of course, was before televised opera got underway', says Victoria, 'so our broadcasts played a very important part in popularising opera, particularly among young people who might otherwise never have considered it as a form of entertainment which they could afford and enjoy.'

The illusion that opera was an expensive and recondite diversion for the establishment had been fostered by three generations of culture-hungry rich New Yorkers. The Met itself had orginally been owned by its box holders, who leased it to the management. It is not surprising, therefore, that the audiences were regarded as among the most conservative in the world. John Lennon's injunction to a Royal Variety Show audience, 'If you don't feel like applauding, just rattle your jewellery', might well have been applied to the opera-goers at the Met, even in the early 'fifties. Their responses, however, were increasingly enlivened by the 'standees' who queued for cheap tickets and stood throughout the performances. Bing was very careful to insist on ensemble rather than solo curtain calls for fear that the standees might form a noisy and enthusiastic fan-club for any one performer.

Another characteristic feature of the rickety but ever-so-respectable opera house and of New York society was the practice of organising benefit performances in aid of worthy causes. The city's *grandes dames* derived solace and large sums of money from such nights, devoted to causes such as the 'Free Milk Fund for Babies'.

'It was a whole new world for me, and I must admit that I enjoyed it thoroughly. The public was so warm and thoughtful. There was one girl, for example, who used to send a little angel backstage at every performance that she attended. Nothing expensive—just a little figure from a department store—but it was always different.

'At the time, we were living in an apartment in a hotel on the Avenue of the Americas. There was quite an opera colony there—Martinelli, Renata Tebaldi, Giuseppe di Stefano, Mario del Monaco. It was very convenient because although we could eat in the restaurant, it was a proper, self-contained apartment which we could treat like home. You can never really feel at home in hotel rooms. Over the years, we went back there again and again until at last it went downhill and everybody moved out.

The Spring tour was a colourful, if gruelling experience. Over three hundred members of the Met's one thousand-strong staff took opera to the citizens of the United States. Two trains, accommodating twenty-five people per baggage car, travelled thousands of exhausting miles. Bing was always very anxious that music-lovers outside New York should see representative Met productions, not mere poor-quality copies. It was therefore a provision of his contracts that his stars should tour as well as performing during the season itself.

Travel imposes peculiar strains, cramped travel still more. Victoria was rather shocked by the company's method of passing the time. 'Gossip,' she says, 'seemed often to serve as a source of amusement. We used to meet each day in the dining car, and one day, a colleague joined us for a meal but elected to leave before coffee. Everyone was nice to her while she was there, but as soon as she had left, they all got together and simply tore her to pieces. I'd never heard such vitriolic talk. It made me feel very ill and uneasy. Eventually, Enrique and I went to Mr Bing and obtained special permission to travel by air. We'd noticed unpleasantness like this during the actual season in New York, but I'd always been able to escape by retreating to my dressing-room with my crochet or with a book. On these long journeys across America there was no escape. In general, I find that the public has a mistaken idea of the amount of contact that normally exists between performing artists. Because they see a number of "names" billed together time after time, they assume that we live in one another's pockets. It's not true. As a rule, we meet on stage, say good-night after the performance, and that's that. At the Met, I hope that I was on good terms with everyone, but there were no intimate friendships.'

Within a few weeks of her first performance of *Madam Butterfly*, Victoria was singing the role at Covent Garden. She followed her usual practice of giving a recital first—this time at the Royal Festival Hall, which had opened only the month before as part of the Festival of Britain.

The warmth of her reception at Covent Garden abashed and delighted Victoria. She gave a series of performances of *Butterfly* and *La Bohème* which were in repertoire with Covent Garden's own Festival Opera—Vaughan Williams' *The Pilgrim's Progress*. The London *Times,* usually renowned for its reserve, showed no trace of the British *sang froid* in its response to the Butterfly:

> Miss Victoria de los Angeles returned to Covent Garden last night to give one of those great performances around which legends grow. The quality of her singing came as no surprise—and yet so subtle were her nuances of phrase, so beautiful and effortless was her flow of tone and so boundless her sympathy that even those passages worn threadbare by familiarity were like cloth of gold. But the real revelation of the evening was her acting as Butterfly. Since her first appearance in this theatre as Mimì she has opened out from bud into full flower and her penetrating psychological insight into the young heart newly awakened to love succeeded in transforming what was conceived as a mere magazine story into the realms of great tragedy. It would be difficult to imagine an interpretation in which music and drama were more close. Moved by Miss de los Angeles' performance, every-

one else, both on the stage and in the orchestra pit, made a gallant effort to be worthy of her. Miss Monica Sinclair's Suzuki was again outstanding as also were the sensitivity and pliancy of the orchestral playing under Mr Warwick Braithwaite.

The long, thin cast lists, known as 'snakes' which the old Met used to issue give a vivid picture of the closing days of Bing's first season. In the last weeks of March and the beginning of April 'the snakes' in fact show that the Met public was enjoying performances by one of the century's great dramatic sopranos in the final phase of her career just as a new lyric soprano was taking off. Kirsten Flagstad was singing Leonora in *Fidelio,* Isolde and Brunnhilde in the same weeks as Victoria was debuting with Marguerite, Mimì and Butterfly. It was a fascinating juxtaposition of the old and the new opera worlds which had come about because Bing was determined that Flagstad, then 55, should be heard once more at the Met before her official retirement the following year. Victoria, whose recital debut outside the Spanish peninsula had been the previous year in Flagstad's native Oslo where she had in fact been hailed as a 'new Kirsten Flagstad' now found herself singing side by side with the real Flagstad.

'I shall always remember her with gratitude and affection,' says Victoria. 'She wrote me such a lovely letter of congratulation and encouragement when I first appeared in New York. It is not the sort of thing a young artist can expect from such a great senior, and I cherish it so much I keep it framed in my studio at home over the piano. You can hear the simple warmth of Flagstad's personality in her voice if you listen. It is all there.'

When Victoria returned to the Met for the 1952–3 season, it was to sing the Countess in a refurbished production of *The Marriage of Figaro.* She kept her public waiting for their favourite de los Angeles role, alternating *Figaro, Manon* and *Bohème,* sometimes with Björling, sometimes with di Stefano until late in the season, when again she returned to *Butterfly.* The tour in April and May was the most ambitious that the

Met had undertaken in fifty years, even taking in the major Canadian venues.

Her fame as an interpreter of *Butterfly* had spread so fast and so wide that she was forced to start her third season with a whole cluster of performances as Cio Cio San. These were followed by Micaela in *Carmen*, Eva in *Die Meistersinger* and, of course, Mimì in *Bohème*. These productions reflected both the successes of the new regime at the theatre and the difficulties that Bing and his company were undergoing. As Eva, for example, Victoria wore new costumes specially designed and made up in the Met's workshops. The sets, however, dated from 1923. *La Bohème*, however, had been a totally new English language production. The populist approach, even so, can be carried too far. An English *Die Fledermaus* was a runaway success. An English *Bohème*, staged à la Broadway, was a dismal failure. The original Italian libretto was quickly restored and the production toned down.

Such failures made Bing understandably cautious. New productions demanded a budget of $40,000–$75,000. A revamped production, on the other hand, with a big star like Victoria as the draw, cost no more than $20,000. Considering that her name now packed audiences in, the Met's top fee of $1,000 per performance for its singers seems a fair investment. While acknowledging that an opera singer's life is not a long one and must therefore be well remunerated, Bing was always very much aware that his top fee was not comparable with the sort of earnings which Victoria could make by concert and recital fees, nor even with the *prima's* fee in Vienna or at La Scala. He was therefore very anxious to do all that he could to ensure that Victoria would continue to commit herself to these two-month seasons during this make-do-and-mend period.

When once the performances at the Met were over, Victoria did not stay in New York for long. 'I was overawed by the sheer grandeur, variety and size of the country,' she says, 'and I came to love the American people as I made my recital tours. In turn, they seemed to be rather overawed by the traditions of Europe. Unfortunately, I only ever had a superficial sort of dressing-room relationship with any of them, so I never had a chance to talk to them much. At the time, you know, I always dressed in black. I had become rather plump, and hoped that the black would conceal it. But looking back now, I feel that that black was representative of my life in those years. It established me as somehow apart from the rest of the world, like the black of a nun's habit or even the black of a singer's dress when she is on the platform. I travelled a great deal, but never went anywhere, if you know what I mean. It now seems to me a great pity that I didn't try to brighten up this gloomy, cocooned sort of life. I could have gone to the homes of so many people and could have had wonderful and fascinating relationships with them. People had such a wrong impression of me. They thought I was grand because I did not approach people, but really it was just a question of feeling shy. I also needed a great deal of time to be alone in order to concentrate on my work and my career.

'I could have become close friends with somebody like Tebaldi, whom I admired very much from afar. I think we would have got on very well if I had not been so withdrawn. I was never envious of other singers, and this is what usually makes friendships impossible in the opera world.'

At the opening of Victoria's fourth season, she was preparing for two new productions. *Faust,* directed by Peter Brook, opened the season on November 16, and *Pélleas and Mélisande* followed soon afterwards. Victoria had long wanted to sing Mélisande, and had urged it upon a reluctant Bing.

Brook had established something of a reputation as an *enfant terrible* during his tenure of the post as resident producer at Covent Garden. Since his announcement that he was going to update *Faust* from its usual mediaeval setting to the nineteenth century, there had been mutterings of outrage and trepidation among New York's music lovers. Pierre Monteux, who was to conduct the new production, dissociated himself from the controversy by announcing, 'As a musician, I concern myself only with the music.' Victoria shared this view until the final stages of the rehearsals. For her first appearance, the designer provided a figure-hugging dress of daffodil yellow. 'Generally, I was too afraid to upset anybody, but I just took one look at that thing and said, "No! I will not go out there looking like a canary!" Thank heavens, everyone else agreed and a replacement costume in dull blue was run up.

'Working with Peter Brook was a very strange experience. I always felt somehow that he was learning—perhaps "exploring" would be a better word—to see how to make singers act. Sometimes he would make us do movement exercises or sit on the floor at the most awkward moments—extraordinary things like that. "Please, Mr Brook," we would implore him, "don't make us sit down now. It really is going to be rather difficult to get up *and* maintain a note just at this moment." Björling and I lost many a battle that way. Of course, we realised that he was a very good director but thought that his ideas worked better in straight theatre than in opera.'

In the event, Brook's transposition worried no one. Victoria's nineteenth-century costumes and the top hat and opera cloak worn by Mephistopheles passed without comment. There was, too, an especially warm welcome for Monteux. He was now approaching eighty and making his return to the Met after an absence of thirty-five years as resident conductor of the San Francisco Symphony Orchestra. The Met had sorely felt the lack of a world-class conductor, and Monteux solved that problem in his three-year stay. The Met was going up in the world.

For Victoria, the greatest reward of this season was the performance of *Pélleas and Mélisande*: 'It is not an opera with a very wide following. You need a musically-cultivated audience. The sort of audience which looks for dramatic top notes and bravura displays of virtuosity is going to be disappointed. Mélisande herself is a very strange character. You can only really understand her by a very close study of the poetry. It's a subtle character, not one that you can use to show off your own personality.'

Bing was surprised and delighted by the success of the new

opera. One critic wrote that 'when her voice was at its sweetest, as it was in the Tower scene, nothing else seemed to matter in the world.' Others commended her loveliness and slenderness in the role. That says a lot for the extent to which she had projected herself into the part, for her chubbiness had become an affectionate standing joke with the company.

'I hated the whole business of weight', she says, 'and tried to think tall and thin. I suppose I must have had some success, because people always used to come backstage and say, "Oh, I thought you were *much* taller." That always made me very sad, because I had been very thin until I was twenty-two or twenty-three and began to sing a lot more. I haven't the right bones or the right constitution to carry a lot of weight, and whenever I see a doctor, the first thing he ever says is, "You *must* lose weight." It's an occupational hazard, of course, and at least in the theatre it does not matter so much so long as you project an aura of elegance.'

That 1953–4 season, which Victoria ranks among the most exciting of her life, ended with a performance of *The Barber of Seville*. She was glad to be able to demonstrate the full range of her talents in Mozart's and Rossini's different accounts of the same character. There is much flirtatious fun in Rossini's Rosina as she is pursued by the Count, whereas Mozart's Rosina, once caught and wedded and bedded, is a noble but tragic figure.

All in all, it would have been the perfect season, had it not been for one continuing source of frustration. The new production of *Carmen*, directed by Tyrone Guthrie, opened to good reviews that year. Victoria played Micaela. She was sure that she should, and could, play Carmen.

'Mr Bing always saw me as a shy, sweet sort of person, and just could not imagine me playing Carmen, so I was always put down to sing docile little Micaela. I hate to say this, but I really do think that he was very short-sighted in this. Just because you are shy in real life, it doesn't mean that you cannot be extrovert and confident on stage. The best comedians are usually terribly dull, unhappy people in real life, but on stage they make you die laughing.'

There was, of course, much other business to be dealt with, but Victoria left all telephone calls, letters, telegrams and problems with managements and press to Enrique. She simply cut herself off from all the practical problems of her career. If Enrique was not there to open letters or to answer the telephone, letters remained unopened, the telephone unanswered. Victoria's attitude to her husband was every bit as submissive as that of her mother to her father. She rarely questioned his decisions.

Apart from occasional gala occasions, Victoria led a remarkably isolated life. For all that, she was now a worldwide star, most of her evenings were spent alone at home, and she looked forward to those galas like a country girl to a coming-out dance.

One of the few people with whom Victoria made contact on a social occasion during these years was King Mohamed V of Morocco. Perhaps he, too, was lonely while surrounded by people. Whatever the cause, when the King was brought by Mayor Lindsay of New York to a supper reception after the performance, he and Victoria sat down together and chatted happily about their lands and their families into the small hours. It was after a charity gala of *La Traviata*, and the reception was held in the restaurant inside the Met itself which really came into its own on such occasions.

Kings and supper receptions played a small part in her life, however. Now that she could afford champagne, she had little time to drink it. She felt that she had a special rapport with two other singers, Marian Anderson and Licia Albanese, but they, of course, were too busy to afford more than occasional relief from the solitude and the hard work which constituted the mainstays and central features of her existence.

Marian Anderson, the black mezzo-soprano who gave 'soul' a meaning in classical music, was born in Philadelphia in 1902. She was without peer in her field by the time Victoria came to know her in the 'fifties. She remains without peer or challenger.

Anderson had been at Victoria's Carnegie Hall debut, and

had congratulated Sol Hurok on bringing a great artist to New York. When this message was passed on, Victoria was deeply moved. She had long admired Anderson's singing and, as she says, 'It is so very rare for a senior established artist—and there was no artist as senior and established as Marian—to be so welcoming and gracious to a newcomer.'

Like Victoria, Anderson led a busy life as a recitalist, but at last, in the 1954–5 season, she came to the Met to sing Ulrica in Verdi's *Un ballo in maschera*. She was the first featured black performer ever to appear there. In his autobiography, Rudolf Bing speaks with pride of that historic evening and observes drily that the Metropolitan Opera Board was not among the many organisations which sent letters and telegrams of support and congratulations.

'I saw a lot of Marian then,' Victoria remembers. 'We were both on the same programme when there was a special with President Truman's daughter Margaret. Poor Margaret! She sat there totally transfixed as we talked shop. I have never discussed singing with anyone as much as with Marian. She was an almost mystic force. What Toscanini was to conducting, she was to singing. I admired her for the simplicity of her approach to singing. Like me, she sang from the heart or not at all. She was also an extraordinarily supportive and generous colleague. I don't believe that anyone has ever sung spirituals with the same power as she brought to them. Her singing of them gave me an insight into America and American history such as I never acquired either from books or from my extensive touring of the country. You could feel it all, hear it all, the torment and the vigour of that great, great country.'

Licia Albanese had been a resident artist at the Met since the 'thirties, when she came over from Bari to live in America. She had married the stockbroker Joseph Gimma, and soon established herself as one of the most popular, uncomplicated and un-prima-donna-ish members of the company. Victoria was gradually taking on the roles that Albanese was beginning to relinquish, but she showed no sign of resentment towards the new star. 'On the contrary, she was a very kind and well-loved singer. Enrique and I only met them both socially, however, when we dined together after a charity performance organized by Lucrezia Bori.'

But otherwise, Victoria returned each night from the glamour and glitter of the Opera House to an empty apartment. She found it difficult to sleep these days, so she took to going to bed very late and arising after midday. By that time, Enrique had long since left the apartment to conduct the day's business.

'I rarely went out on my own, but stayed at home to work, much as I would have done if I had been living a more conventional life in Spain. But, of course, this was not a Spanish house. It was a hotel apartment in the middle of one of the world's greatest and busiest cities. I had no children yet, and Enrique had his own work to do, so I felt the loneliness very much. I didn't have a brother or somebody like that to take me out, so I spent the time studying my music.

'I was talking to some friends of Maria Callas the other day, and they told me that when Maria arrived at the Met her first question was, "Tell me, what is Victoria really *like*?" No-one could tell her. I had this reputation for being remote, deliberately distant, you know? Nothing could have been further from the truth. It was just that, as soon as I stopped singing, I disappeared. Nobody knew what happened to me, and I was never to be seen in the restaurants and night clubs. I was just working alone at home. They only knew me on stage. Nobody ever found out what my views were, what I felt about anything.

'It was ridiculous, really. I was leading two totally separate lives. Victoria de los Angeles, opera star, public figure—"the healthy girl of the Met", they used to call me—and Victoria Magriña, unglamorous, hardworking woman like any other. It seems extraordinary now. I might do things very differently if I had my life to live over again.

'For entertainment I had an upright piano in the apartment. The Met supplied those to all their singers. I used to play it for pleasure and, of course, in preparation for new roles. I tried to go to the museums, but it went against all my

111

experience and conditioning to go on my own. So, whenever Enrique and I had time *together* we would go out to explore these and the art galleries. I ought to have gone more often. I love paintings and I remember seeing one Cézanne of flowers and being reduced to tears by it. But I was so inhibited that I hardly ever returned.

'Sometimes I went shopping. I always dressed very simply, just wanting to be normal and anonymous as I would have been had I indeed been a Spanish housewife. Once I went to buy some face powder, and the assistant showed me several varieties. When she got to the most expensive, she looked at me pityingly and said, "Have a look at these. They are fabulously expensive and, of course, you'd never be able to afford them, but just look!"

'I duly looked and went away. The next day, I went back to the same store, but this time I was wearing some jewellery and I went in the persona of Victoria de los Angeles.

'"Madame," said a different assistant, "here is just the powder for you", and she pulled out a sample of that very powder which the other girl had described as far too expensive for me. I thought it was funny at the time, but now it seems just another rather sad reflection of the totally divided life that I was leading.'

To Americans, reading of Victoria's triumphs at the Met and her coast-to-coast progresses in concert and recital programmes across their country, it must have seemed that she had now adopted their country exclusively. Yet hardly were her Met seasons and tours completed than she was winging off all over the world—one moment singing *Bohème* in Rio, the next *Freischütz* in Milan and then on to Buenos Aires for *Madam Butterfly*, coming back to Europe for *Lohengrin* at Covent Garden.

To her fans, life in those years seemed an endless succession of bravoing audiences. 'But,' says Victoria, 'behind it all there were enormous ups and downs. You cannot travel so far without ever having any problems, can you? When you are away in other countries things happen that you cannot possibly foresee. For instance, just at the time I had my big

112

success at the Colón Theatre in Buenos Aires in 1952, Eva Peron had died. I was down to do a number of performances of *Manon* and *Butterfly*. But everything in Argentina was suddenly closed. There were no trains, no restaurants, nothing at all. It was a very delicate situation. I did not want to disappoint the public but I did not want to offend anybody either. Enrique and I got in touch with the Embassy and we told them that after what had happened we thought that we had better cancel and move on. But they begged us to stay and even suggested that we move into the Embassy for the time being. We decided to remain in our hotel and in the end we were able to honour the contract. I was so glad because the Argentinians were such wonderful audiences. They did really love me at the Colón and I think I gave some of my best performances there because I was so relaxed and happy with them. When I first went there they even invaded the dressing-rooms, and the police had to be called in to calm everybody down. Such warmth makes it possible for you to sing in a way you did not think you ever could. When I went back to the Colón I always felt that I was "going home" again just as I did when I went back for many years to the Granada Festival in Spain for recitals and performances of *La vida breve*. At both I felt a part of me belonged there because I made such wonderful contact with the public during the performances.

'Sometimes when I was travelling I had to fight to establish that contact because I had such bad luck in getting there. When I went on from Buenos Aires to Mexico there was a whole series of disasters. I was delayed in leaving Argentina, the engines of the plane were thought unsafe and we were held up for repairs. Some of my jewellery disappeared. And when I arrived I had to go straight from the plane to the Opera House to sing *Manon*, *Faust*, *Bohème* and *Butterfly* in a week. It was madness. And it was particularly hard because you are so high up in Mexico City and you have to adjust to breathing in that altitude. But they said I won through in the end. I did want to please them, to sing at my best for them—even if the performances meant to be given over 15 days were crammed into one week.'

Although Victoria spent much time in America in the 1950s, she in fact made a number of appearances in the winter months

113

at La Scala in Milan. When, for example, she sang Agatha in *Der Freischütz* in 1955, not only did she get a warm welcome from the Milanese but also an insistent invitation from the Scala management for her to be involved in the first season of the theatre's new offshoot, the 600-seat Piccola Scala to be opened in December.

Victoria agreed when she went back to the main Scala auditorium for the end of the 1954–55 season to take over Rosina in *Il barbiere di Siviglia*. Callas had had a sensational season in the same auditorium that year with her Medea. But Rosina did not seem to suit her. Victoria took over and was a huge success in the part. But she wanted to avoid getting involved in the sort of rivalry that existed at that time between the supporters of Callas and Tebaldi. Victoria says, 'It was my first Italian role at the Scala and that was all that mattered. I wanted them to like me for that.

'But what I really enjoyed about Milan was working with the director Margherita Wallmann for the Piccola with *Mitridate Eupatore*. Wallmann had trained as a ballet dancer in Vienna but had to give it up after an accident. She had a wonderful sense of movement and I learned a lot from her as did Maria Callas who was directed by her in *Medea*.

Although the working conditions were cramped at the Piccola, Victoria thoroughly enjoyed the studio approach Wallmann had to adopt at the Piccolo in order to bring back to life Alessandro Scarlatti's neglected masterpiece. The demands of Victoria's career did not allow her to work in this comparatively rarefied world for long. Next time, when she slipped out of America to return to Italy it was to do the big popular works in her repertoire in Rome, Naples and Sicily. 'I was doing the big popular works of the Italian repertoire—*Bohème* and *Butterfly* in Italy—but I was not nervous. If I had gone thinking, "Oh dear, I wonder what the Italians will think of me, a Spanish soprano in Puccini", I would have been lost. I thought, "I will show them how to sing Mimì and Butterfly." I had to prove a Spanish soprano could do it.

The 1954–5 season in New York was devoted to the consolidation of Victoria's previous successes, rather than to the breaking of new ground. On November 8th, the season started with a televised evening of opera extracts in which Victoria sang Mimì to Richard Tucker's Rodolfo in Act I of *La Bohème*. She then sang a series of *Manon*s and *Faust*s, repeated her triumphant *Butterfly* and then made a flying visit to Milan to sing Agatha in *Der Freischütz* at La Scala before returning to New York for yet more *Faust*s and *Butterfly*s. The televised gala, a Saturday afternoon broadcast of *Manon*, and continued nationwide tours established Victoria's name with a public far wider than that of most opera singers.

The 1955–6 season was also devoted to tried and tested parts which had proved so successful. But the time had come to move on. The public was informed that she would be taking eighteen months leave of absence in order to tour Italy, Austria, France and London and to fulfil a booking for a three-month tour of Australia and New Zealand.

Victoria was thirty-three years old. She had been acclaimed as Mimì, Marguerite, Rosina, the Countess Almaviva and the definitive Butterfly. Not bad for a singer who had sought to be recognised as 'a recitalist who also sang opera'. But for all her success as a performer, Victoria had been brought up with other ambitions, other needs. These had been disregarded over the years at considerable cost. Even with singing, she would often feel incomplete. She needed something more than a celebrated life of solitude in a New York apartment. It was to be many years before she could put a name to that something.

12

Victoria returned to the Met in November 1957 to find
things much changed. That new broom which Bing had
started wielding in the 1950–2 seasons had had its effect.
New York's greatest opera house now boasted a complete
selection of new or totally refurbished productions. Victoria
started the new season with her first ever performance as
Violetta in *La Traviata*. It was a wonderful, romantic, colourful confection by Tyrone Guthrie which had first been
seen the year before, starring Tebaldi. The *Faust* which now
she sang with Nicolai Gedda was the new Peter Brook
production which had occasioned such a stir at the opening
of her 1953–4 season. *The Barber of Seville* and *The Marriage of Figaro* had been dusted down so that Victoria could
once more present her contrasting portraits of Rosina, but
this time without competition from creaking sets and tatty
costumes.

'Of course, Rossini's and Mozart's conceptions of the
character of Rosina are totally different. In the Mozart, you
have always to remember that you are a countess. The
approach has to be very much more poised and dignified
than with Rossini's odd, funny little Rosina. It is no bad
thing to think as you sing Rosina that one day you are going

to be the Countess, but it's very difficult as you play the Countess to think that she could ever have been Rosina.'

The innovations had not been made without some objections from performers. Tebaldi, for example, had politely but firmly rejected several of the new departures introduced by Guthrie into *La Traviata*, while Callas had been scathing in her criticism both of sets and of costumes. The new production, therefore, for all its glittering surface, was by now somewhat less than unified in nature or intent. She was rehearsed in the new part not by Guthrie, of course, but by an assistant who had learned the necessary business by participation in the rehearsal the previous year.

Victoria was therefore confronted by a twofold challenge. She must bring the production back to life and give it coherence by realising a character which she found—at least, as compared to those other roles that she had successfully played—alien to her nature. 'I could not find much of Violetta in myself', she confesses, 'but I had to try. I did not want to continue repeating a handful of roles in which I had enjoyed success. Worst of all, nobody would give me Carmen, which I still longed to do.

The opportunity to record *Carmen* was not to occur until the late 'sixties, but by 1957, when she returned to New York, Victoria had already established an impressive list of eight complete opera record credits. She was immediately asked to add her *Traviata* to the others, and recorded it two years later in the Rome Opera House. Once again, she was lucky in that she was one of the top opera stars in the world at the moment when the commercial recording industry was just coming into its own, and producers were hungry for talent.

The boom in gramophone sales also served to interest music-lovers who might otherwise have disregarded opera. Houses were packed, and Victoria's name reached a very much larger public than that which her predecessors had commanded.

With the old 78 rpm records, you had to change the record after each aria, and a complete recording of, say, *Butterfly,* would have weighed a ton and taken hours to listen to from start to finish. Now you could buy the complete opera in a two- or three-record set. At last, a certain amount of the drama of opera could be conveyed on record. You could sit down, close your eyes and imagine. It did an enormous amount of good to opera, which, of course, has always been a minority interest, but never more so than in the years immediately after the introduction of films and television.

'Actually, television, too, was now playing its part in the popularisation of opera. NBC televised a nineteen-minute excerpt from our *Traviata* that year, and I began to notice how many young people were turning up at the opera house all of a sudden. I think that these newcomers, more than any other factor, helped to make those hoary old productions unaccept-able. They were used to high standards in the cinema and on Broadway and, having learned to love opera through records and through broadcasts, they saw no reason why they should put up with moth-eaten convention at the Met.'

The new interest in opera created an increased demand for the services of leading singers. The Lyric Opera of Chicago, founded in 1954 by Carol Fox, was constantly seeking new box-office draws, and, just as Victoria arrived at the beginning of the 1957–8 season, a young impresario named Lawrence Kelly was enlisting the aid of Maria Callas in launching the sumptuous new 4,100-capacity theatre at Dallas. Both solicited Victoria's aid. Meanwhile the San Francisco Opera, generally regarded as second only to the Met, had acquired a new, dynamic director in Kurt Herbert Adler on the death of Gaetano Merola, the founder director. Adler, too, eagerly urged Victoria to sing with his company.

For the moment, however, Victoria was too happy to be back to consider such inveiglements. 'It was, after all, the nearest thing to home that I had just then,' she says. 'We had just been back to stay with my parents at the old family home in Barcelona, and I found it very difficult to acclimatise from one world to the other. Like those two identities of mine, they were a long, long way apart. Once I had re-adapted to the pace of home life in Barcelona, of course, I found it still more difficult to get back into the New York routine and I missed

119

Spain terribly. Back there, I had gone back to being Vittorina, the caretaker's daughter and had left Victoria de los Angeles behind. As soon as I climbed back into the plane for New York—still a twenty-hour flight—I was thinking just one thing, 'At least it's not too long till I can come back for Christmas.' Then I just set my jaw and tried to will myself into the person of Victoria de los Angeles again.

'It was back to the old routine. I lived for the rehearsals and the performances and, in the long term, for the vague prospect of returning to Spain.'

If in the past Victoria had been able to shut out all thoughts of Spain, her family and her youthful illusions and ambitions, she now found it impossible. Not only did her life seem increasingly empty and friendless save when she was singing, but her father was very ill. Her recent visit to Spain had been further saddened by the attitude of the Liceo public to her when she returned at the height of her powers in her most-loved opera role, Butterfly. Disenchantment had set in with a radio interview on the eve of the performance. 'Why', asked the interviewer, 'have you forgotten and neglected Barcelona?' Spiritedly Victoria came back with the words, 'I have *never* forgotten Barcelona. And I think I have done more for the city singing all over the world than I would ever have done by staying here in Spain.' The truth was that Victoria had simply not been invited back to the Liceo, not that she was too busy or unwilling to return. It was certainly odd that the Liceo management fostered the impression that Victoria was too busy to return without actually giving her the opportunity to do so.

Today the Spanish public have forgiven her, and Victoria has received numerous Spanish honours, including the *Medalla de la Provincia* from the Barcelona authorities, but at the time it seemed that the Liceo public who had so adored her in the early days of her career could not accept her subsequent international life. Because Butterfly was the role that she had come to be identified with elsewhere all over Europe, it was a particularly emotional moment for her when she sang it for the first time in her home opera house where

120

(*Above*) Victoria (centre) with Richard Lewis and Elisabeth Schwarzkopf in San Francisco's *Don Giovanni*

(*Right*) At the piano in her New York apartment in the 1950s

(*Above*) The Vienna Boys Choir
surprise Victoria on stage at the Met
on Christmas Eve 1957

(*Opposite top*) Backstage at the
Metropolitan with Rudolf Bing

(*Opposite bottom*) Dining with King
Mohamed V of Morocco after a charity
gala in New York

(*Right*) Victoria with Lord Harewood
whom she came to know through her
many recital performances at the
Edinburgh Festival under his direction

(*Above*) At the Trevi fountain—
Victoria with Jussi Björling in Rome
where they recorded her second
Butterfly shortly before his death

(*Left*) With Pierre Monteux who
conducted Victoria in French operas
like *Pélleas et Mélisande* at the Met
and, later, in a famous recording of
Manon

(Top) Victoria and the Queen Mother; *(below)* with Prince Juan Carlos

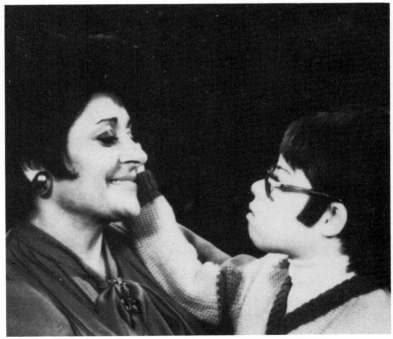

(*Above*) Signing autographs during a successful 1960s recital tour in Europe

(*Right*) Victoria at the Festival of Granada, a 'second home' for her where she gave recitals throughout the 1950s, '60s and '70s and still sings there today

(*Opposite*) Victoria with her two sons: (*above*) Juan Enrique, born in 1963, (*below*) Alejandro, born in 1965

(*Above*) Receiving the Golden Medal of her home city of Barcelona, one of the many honours that began to come Victoria's way in the 1960s

(*Right*) Victoria, the only woman to have received the Spanish honour of the Ribbon of Alfonso X, El Sabio

her opera career had begun. She was therefore totally unprepared for the almost palpable hostility that seemed to hang over the evening. As the performance wore on Victoria's heart sank so low, only the mumbled encouragement of Anna Maria Canali who was singing Suzuki enabled her to get through it. She was the city's prodigal son come home but she was being received in silence.

'That was my last visit to my childhood home,' she recalls, 'because my father had at last had to retire from his post at the university and my parents had moved into the little house that I had bought for them in the early 'fifties. It was a terrible wrench for them. Retirement was an idea totally alien to my father. He'd never have given up from choice. He still went back to the university every day to talk to his old friends.'

But for all her worries, Victoria kept the same thought constantly in her mind. Like a schoolgirl, 'Not long now till Christmas. Not long now. . . .'

Then disaster struck. Renata Tebaldi had been accompanied throughout her working life by her mother, Giuseppina. They were inseparable. In the frequently lonely, globetrotting life of the singer, Giuseppina had supplied support and companionship. At the end of November, Giuseppina Tebaldi died.

Renata was inconsolable. She cancelled her season at the Met.

Bing reshuffled performances in order to bridge the gap left by her absence, but there remained one very important evening for which he was compelled to ask Victoria's assistance. It was a gala performance of *Traviata* in which Tebaldi had been billed to appear. It was on Christmas Eve.

Victoria agreed to help the Met by taking Tebaldi's place. She telephoned her parents and explained the situation to Bernardo. 'I'll be back in the New Year,' she promised, 'and I am so, so sorry not to be able to get there for Christmas. But you do understand, don't you? Please understand. . . .'

Victoria's parents understood and said they would look forward to seeing her all the more in the New Year.

On December 24, Victoria was greeted on stage by a tremendous ovation. Christmas Eve is always magical, and tonight was no exception. The performance went better than ever. The audience was ebullient. Exhausted but elated, as always after a good performance, Victoria sat in the dressing-room with the applause at the end of each act still ringing in her ears.

There was a knock at the door.

'Come in!' She tried to compose herself rapidly.

It was Bing. His face was impassive, his voice stern. 'Would you mind accompanying me back to the stage, please, Victoria?'

'Now?'

'Immediately.'

'Well, all right . . .' Victoria was bemused. She kept asking as she followed him, 'What's wrong, Mr Bing? What's all this about?'

He did not speak. The stage was in pitch darkness. Victoria peered through the dark and made out an unusually large army of stage-hands mustered there. Suddenly, she was dazzled by brilliant light. The side and the front stage-lights went up, though the curtain remained down.

There was a Christmas tree on stage. The Vienna Boys Choir, which happened to be touring in New York at the time, were gathered upstage. This, Bing said, was a gift of thanks from the Met. And when the applause on stage had died down, and Victoria had wiped the mist from her eyes, she and the choir sang Christmas in with carols.

'It was a wonderful moment,' Victoria smiles at the memory, 'a moment in which artist, company, and the management all seemed to be part of one enormous family. Since I was missing my family so much at the time, it really helped, even though it made me very tearful. It was also very good to see how much I mattered to the Metropolitan and how pleased they were to have me back.'

Victoria now had to complete a short concert tour during January before she could at last return to Barcelona. In Phoenix, Arizona, she received a telegram stating in cruelly succinct terms, that her father was dead.

She arrived in Barcelona just two days later. Red-eyed from crying, she had not slept on the journey and was in a state of shock. When the plane landed it was raining and cold. Victoria stepped down from the plane to see her family waiting for her—a small group of figures dressed in black. There was just time for her to see her father's body before the coffin was nailed up and laid in the earth.

That night she wandered again the old haunts of her childhood; the university gardens where she and Bernardo had walked in the dawn; the room where she had discovered her first, abandoned piano; the flat where they had lived for so long and where her father had exhorted her to entertain visitors, 'Sing, Victoria, sing!' Victoria was now thirty-five years old. She had seen things and done things which many a young girl might consider enviable, 'But as I walked around the university buildings and thought about my father's life, I thought, "Here are you, thirty-five, blessed with a good voice and capacity for work which have made you successful. But what have *you* done in all those years? Victoria de los Angeles has achieved a lot, but *you*? Have you done anything important?"'

There were, of course, practical problems to be resolved. Victoria's mother was the first. In the early years, she had travelled everywhere with Victoria. Could she not now come to New York? The invitation was not, of course, without self-interest. Victoria would have been grateful for her mother's commonsense attitude to life and for her company. Her mother answered that perhaps later she would like to travel with Victoria again. For the time being, however, she just wanted to stay very quietly in Barcelona with all the people and things which she and Bernardo had always loved. She wanted to stay with Pepe for what was originally intended to be a short spell, but she was to stay there for most of the rest of her life, devoting herself to the care of her grandchildren.

Victoria returned to America aware that her last avenue of retreat was now gone. Barcelona had represented real life to her, and peace when all else seemed frantic and futile. Her grief at the loss of her father was intensified by her guilt that she had not been by his side when he died. She had been hiding in her work for a long time now, and now she threw herself into it with a vengeance. In the eighth week of the season, she sang Desdemona in Verdi's *Otello* with Mario del Monaco in the title role and Leonard Warren as Iago. To end the season, she repeated *Butterfly*, but this time, in a new production with Bergonzi as her Pinkerton.

The innocence and trusting nature of Desdemona lay readily within Victoria's natural dramatic range, and many critics found her performance in *Otello* very moving. Victoria, however, remembers this role with some reservations. 'I don't really think that I was quite right—or maybe I just wasn't quite ready—for the dramatic scenes in the first acts. I only felt really at home in the part in Act IV with the Willow song and the prayer.'

Victoria was convinced that she must keep extending her range if her work was to remain fresh and alive. Bing agreed that new roles were needed but was uncertain as to which she should try next. She was anxious to extend her French repertoire by following *Faust* and *Manon* with Charpentier's *Louise* or *Romeo and Juliet*. Bing disagreed. Victoria therefore committed herself only to the first weeks of the 1958–9 season, when she sang her most famous roles—*Bohème* and *Butterfly*.

1959–60 was her 'French' season, though she still did not obtain permission to sing the new roles that she coveted. After another *Traviata*, she sang *Manon* and *Mélisande* in a revival of the 1954 production. Di Stefano no longer sang at the Met. His attitude to rehearsals for the new productions of *La Bohème* and *Faust* had invoked Bing's wrath. The new resident tenor was Nicolai Gedda. The American audiences soon took the Swedish-born tenor and the Spanish soprano to their hearts and, with the Americans' love of a snappy phrase, dubbed them Vikki and Nikki.

They were well-matched in every way. There was only two years difference in age between them, and, although he had made a later start than she (his international singing compe-

124

tition triumph had not occurred until he was twenty-five), he was a consummate musician and a purist who, like Victoria, eschewed gratuitous *bel canto* fireworks.

Victoria's decision to undertake only half-seasons at the Met gave her more time for her coast-to-coast American recital tours. These were, of course, much more profitable than long engagements at the Met, but the Met would continue to hold a special attraction for her long after she stopped singing there.

Looking back, it is obvious that Victoria's long relationship with the New York Met was undergoing change. There were new decisions about the roles she would play. In discussing what her contribution should be to the 1960–61 season, Victoria again asked that she should play Carmen. Again, Bing would consider her only for the part of Micaela. He had, furthermore, conceived a great desire to present Flotow's *Martha*. Because the action of the opera was set in England, and because Bing was still eager to follow up the success of his English-language *Die Fledermaus*, he saw this as an ideal opportunity to put into practice his theories about opera in English.

Tebaldi had already firmly declined to sing *Eugene Onegin* in English, and now it was Victoria's turn to demur. The role of Lady Harriet Durham was wrong for her, both vocally and temperamentally. It was doubly wrong in a language other than that in which it had been written. Bing was stubborn and persuasive. It would be an entirely new, incomparably lavish production. Carl Ebert would direct. There would be breathtaking costumes and sets by Oliver Smith and the Motley designers. Nino Verchi would conduct. Richard Tucker, she was told, would be her tenor. After some consideration, she finally agreed to sing the role. 'But Lady Harriet was totally wrong for my voice!' says Victoria, in retrospect. 'At the time I accepted it, but now I certainly know better. It was a great mistake.'

She returned to Barcelona for Christmas with her mother, then back to New York in early January for rehearsals. Bing had not exaggerated. The lavish sets included a constantly-flowing waterfall and an amiable, if eccentric, horse called Mathilda. It was lucky for Victoria that she had long since established that she would not sing full out in rehearsals, for the vocal writing was indeed quite wrong for her, and she would certainly never have scored the resounding success which she enjoyed for her performances as Elisabeth in *Tannhäuser* under Georg Solti immediately preceding the opening of *Martha* had her voice been subjected to such unnatural strain.

Martha opened on January 26. Even the horse could not save it. 'In fact, I think that he probably made the best comment on the proceedings', says Victoria. 'He tried to pull us in our little cart into the orchestra pit, which would at least have been one way of stopping the whole fiasco. Otherwise, I can remember very little about *Martha*. I have banished it all from my mind. I begged Mr Bing to release me from my contract, but he would not allow it. He even insisted that I should tour with *Martha*, despite the fact that it was a proven failure. I became so frantic, so ashamed about my performances that I was frequently sick and the understudy had to go on.'

The reviews, at their most generous, spoke of 'a sumptuous waste of talent' and 'a lavish disaster', and complimented the cast on the good humour with which they appeared to ride out the catastrophe. In reality, however, Victoria disliked the opera so much that, at the last, she felt she could not do justice even to the simplest and most melodious of Flotow's arias.

Years later, Bing may have seen his error and accepted the blame. At the time, however, he persisted in his folly. Victoria sang *Martha* through February and March with a few brief escapes into a revival of *La Bohème*. The last of these was on April 10, the last *Martha* three days later. These were her last appearances on the stage of the New York Met.

She had intended to return. She had already initialled the agreement to do so. In discussing future roles, Bing insisted that *Martha* should again be performed, to Victoria's dismay. Even with this in mind, she made her departure with firm plans to return. She did not yet know what change in her own

126

life would end her days with the Met. Just now *Martha* seemed the only stumbling block.

There were no farewells. Victoria had left New York hoping that the problem would be resolved. 'In later years, I had one or two offers from the Met, but due to family commitments nothing came of them, and gradually we lost contact,' says Victoria wistfully. 'Anyhow, it was time I made a move. If I had been given the new roles that I wanted, I would have had a reason to overcome my dislike of being alone, away from my family, but it just wasn't worth it simply in order to play the same old parts again and again.'

Years later, long after the old Met had been pulled down, Victoria saw Bing walking towards her on a New York pavement. 'I thought that he had seen me, but perhaps he had not; he hurried by without a word. I wasn't going to allow that. I went up and buttonholed him. "Mr Bing, how *are* you?" I said. "It's me, Victoria, Victoria de los Angeles!" He nodded acknowledgement, spoke to me briefly and then disappeared.'

13

'It's best to put these things, bluntly, Miss de los Angeles. I am afraid that you will never be able to have a child of your own.'

Victoria just sat and stared wide-eyed at the doctor. She had been married for several years now, and had consulted the doctor with no thought that he might deliver such a verdict. It had never crossed her mind that there could be something wrong with her, that one day she would not be a mother.

'It was a terrible shock,' she remembers, 'a shattering blow to my confidence.'

She can look back on it with a degree of complacency now, but at the time, she found it extraordinarily difficult to accept. By the end of her years at the Met, it had become an accepted if distressing fact. She simply tried not to think about children and attempted to sublimate her needs in work.

And work there was aplenty at the beginning of the 'sixties. It looked as though she might even end up singing more rather than less opera since her departure from the Met. The Argentinians who had responded so warmly to her on her earlier tours urged her to return to the Colon. The great iconoclastic film director, Luis Buñuel, was mounting a new production of *Carmen* in Dallas and regarded Victoria as the ideal interpreter of the role. Meanwhile, she had an opportunity at once to extend her repertoire and to prove her ability as an actress and as a singer. In 1961, she sang at Covent Garden in Zeffirelli's new productions of *Cavalleria rusticana* and *Pagliacci*.

The English audiences and critics, who had hitherto believed Victoria to be a fine singer but a moderate actress, reconsidered when they saw the way in which she threw herself into Zeffirelli's *verismo* productions. She had, in fact, had five days of intensive rehearsal with Zeffirelli. They were needed, for these much-discussed productions were nothing if not complex. They were presented on this occasion as a special gala in aid of the Royal Opera House Benevolent Fund. The Queen Mother rushed back from York, where the Duke and Duchess of Kent were married that day, to attend.

Critics expressed the fear that Victoria would prove too elegant, too aristocratic a performer and that she would either prove too detached or remote for the large streak of vulgarity in Leoncavallo's and Mascagni's scores. As for Victoria, she was rather more afraid of the stage scenery designed for *Cavalleria rusticana*. The sloped angle of the floor area—where the character Santuzza would make her entrance—looked alarmingly risky. Victoria was supposed to run from the highest part of the stage all the way down to the front. 'With that slope and a fast enough run,' she recalls with a laugh, 'there was every chance you could end up in the orchestra pit. It was very frightening.'

Other invitations now started to come in. First, Victoria was asked to sing the world premiere of Falla's *Atlantida* in Barcelona in November 1961. Falla had died before the completion of this opera, and it was later completed by Ernesto Halffter. Then Wieland Wagner offered her a contract to open the 1962 summer season at Bayreuth with a performance of *Tannhäuser*. All in all, despite Victoria's assertion that she derived more joy and satisfaction from her recitals, it now looked as though she was going to spend more and more time in the opera house.

Rudolf Bing had not been the only opera-house manager to have believed in English translations of foreign operas and to have discovered, to his cost, that neither singers nor audiences always liked them. David Webster of Covent Garden had made a similar blunder. After Victoria's triumphant return in January, she was invited to sing Elsa in a new production of *Lohengrin* by Klemperer in 1963. Victoria gladly accepted, but on the condition that the whole production would be in German. She still remembered too vividly her first performances of *Manon, Butterfly* and *Bohème* in London in the early 'fifties. She had sung in the original language while her colleagues had sung back at her in English, a circumstance scarcely conducive to the evocation of romance or the suspension of disbelief.

But then in September, 1961, the impossible happened, and all these plans went awry. 'Despite the original doctor's statement that I could never have a child, I had consulted another doctor some years later, and he told me that it was just possible, provided that I could be patient and would submit to certain treatment. I didn't allow myself to get too excited, but I thought, "Why not?" Then, when I was thirty-eight years old and had almost abandoned all hope, I was suddenly told, "You're going to have a baby!"'

She was happy and hopeful because she felt so well in the first few months of her pregnancy in 1961. She did not cancel any performances. Her Bayreuth, Dallas and London engagements were far enough off to be safe.

'I just could not say that I would not appear in *Atlantida*', she remembers. 'Its premiere was in November—early in my pregnancy—and the Barcelona presentation was to be a concert version conducted by Eduardo Toldra. He had cancer, and was by then a very, very sick old man. He had driven himself so hard to get the work together that he made me feel positively ashamed. He came to my home and talked to me, and he never tried to persuade me not to cancel. He did something far less fair. He inspired me not to cancel. La Scala, you see, had announced a full-scale production of *Atlantida* for 1962, so it was unthinkable that it should not

131

first be performed in Spain. It was also, apparently, unthinkable that I should not be in the cast of that Spanish production because the various performances I had done of *La vida breve* meant that I had become strongly associated with Falla. Anyhow, I just took one look at that brave, committed, kind old man, and I knew that I could not refuse.

'It wasn't as if I had any reason to refuse anyhow. I only had two arias to sing in the opera—it's really an oratorio, a work for chorus, not an opera—and, as I say, it was early in the pregnancy. No one saw any reason why I should not do it. . . .'

Four days before the first performance, Victoria lost her baby.

'It happened so rapidly. One moment, there I was, full of hope and happiness. The next, everything had gone. Everything. And for me, you see, it was everything. It's terrible for anyone to have a miscarriage, but for a thirty-eight-year-old woman who had previously believed that she could never bear children, it was shattering. I felt cheated, because I had come to accept that I couldn't have children. That hadn't been easy, but I had done it, and then my hopes were raised again, and then they were dashed. And there wasn't even hope for the future to buoy me up, or, at least, I didn't think so then. I thought that I would have to continue to be Victoria de los Angeles, the voice, for the rest of my days. The thought that I might not be able to have a child of my own was intolerable to me.

'As for *Atlantida*, I just had to go on with it. It was a great occasion. Prince Juan Carlos was in the audience. No-one else, of course, had prepared my arias or had even heard them before, so there was no question of understudies or anything like that. Either I performed or the whole thing would have to be chalked off. I had no choice. I had a high temperature and could not hold back the tears, but I looked at Toldra, who was so frail that he had fractured a rib whilst conducting, and I thought, "Well, if he can make himself go on, I can find the will to sing." After the performance, I went back to the dressing-room and howled my eyes out. Toldra went home to die.'

Christmas 1961 was far from merry, but friends rallied round. All gave the same advice, 'Get back to work, get on with living. Don't sit around thinking about it.' And Victoria knew that they were right. Once more, her work was her only refuge, and applause the only substitute, however illusory, for the loving need of another.

At the beginning of May, Victoria was back at Covent Garden to sing Mimì to Andre Turp's Pinkerton. Many who remembered her previous performances were disappointed. She was not the same woman who had been there only a few months before, and critics described her as 'oddly frail and small of voice', asserting that her voice was drowned by conductor Edward Downes' flamboyant conception of the score. Victoria hated to disappoint her audiences, and knew that the criticisms were just. She knew, however, that she must persevere. Only through such efforts, however ill-received, would she ever recover her strength and her spirit.

Nothing helped her more than her six-week stay in Bayreuth. Wieland Wagner had assembled a formidable cast for *Tannhäuser*. Apart from Victoria, Grace Bumbry, Wolfgang Windgassen and Dietrich Fischer-Dieskau had been booked for the *Tannhäuser* to beat all *Tannhäusers*.

'In many ways, those were the best artistic conditions in which I have ever worked', she says now. 'Great fellow performers, a superb director and one of the best theatres in the world. Wieland Wagner was wonderful. He put no pressure on me to sing out in rehearsals, and he encouraged me to take things very gently. He never tried to impose his idea of Elisabeth on me. My approach was very—well, very mystical, I suppose—very Spanish, I suppose you could say. I was cautious, of course, about singing before an audience composed entirely of Germans and committed, expert Wagnerians, but this time, I felt sure that I had got the part right. It never occurred to me to be nervous because I knew Elisabeth. She reflected a large part of my own personality. I was very lucky in that I had first sung *Tannhäuser* at the Liceo in Barcelona and there had been no one there to tell me how it should be done. The moves were blocked in, but for the rest, it was up to me to sing the part as I wished. Wieland Wagner respected that. He did not want me to do anything that I did not feel.

'As for the theatre, it's easily the best in the world for Wagner. The acoustics are marvellous and, with half of the orchestra under the stage, the voices are never drowned. The balance is incomparable. Big voices can sail across clear and strong and untrammelled.

'Altogether, it was a lovely time in my life. We took a little villa with a garden. My mother was with us. We prepared our own meals and had total privacy, so it was not like staying in a hotel. There were several days between performances, too, so there were none of the usual pressures involved in cramming rehearsals and performances together. Thank God, we were not allowed to sing anywhere else, so there was no question of dashing off to do recitals here, there and everywhere. We had time to sleep and to explore and to talk. It was a wonderful, wonderful time.'

Then it was back to her loyal audiences in Buenos Aires. They greeted her in a characteristically tumultuous Latin manner. This was the year in which the Colón was granted artistic independence for the first time in fifty-four years. Artists and audiences were intoxicated by their new-found liberty. Victoria sang Rosina in *The Barber of Seville* to applause which swelled and became more insistent with her every entrance and exit. 'There was an audience that really picked you up by the sheer vigour and enthusiasm of their response. It was electric. If I was good that night, the audience must share the credit.'

She sang the part as written. She has always scorned the battery of ornamentation with which most singers drown Rossini's score. 'I have never understood how singers can do that, especially since Rossini himself indicated that it was contrary to his wishes. He once went up to Patti after a performance of the *Barber* and said, "Very nice, but who wrote it?" Good meat needs no sauce, and that vocal line is very good meat. All those embellishments and grace notes destroy that line.'

Later, she sang Mélisande as part of the Colon's special season of French and English operas. It was of a standard unparalleled in the theatre's history. In the past, the best that the Colón had been able to muster had been ill-prepared showcases for stars passing through. Now they had a well-rehearsed, well-conceived production which Victoria today compares favourably with many in which she had performed at the Met.

By October, she was back in opera in America, this time with the San Francisco Company. The managerial policy there in no way constrained Victoria as had the two-month contracts and national tours of the Met. Seasons were shorter and pressures less.

It was having a particularly brilliant fortieth season. Among other artists returning to the War Memorial Opera House that year were Schwarzkopf, Simionato, del Monaco and Gobbi. Zeffirelli was booked to direct, Francesco Molinari Pradel to conduct the orchestra. 'Zeffirelli wasn't actually there,' Victoria remembers. 'We worked with a colleague of his, and I sang three roles, Desdemona, Donna Anna in *Don Giovanni* and Mimì. Everything now seemed to be getting back into the old groove: lots of work, lots of travel, no time to stop and think. I was feeling very well again. When we returned to Barcelona for Christmas that year, there were, of course, a few scars and they still hurt a bit; but basically, Victoria de los Angeles had taken firm control of Vittorina.'

Not for long. In the new year, she went to the doctor complaining of various symptoms. She thought that she recognised them, but was unprepared even to consider that she might be pregnant again for fear of disappointment. 'It's always best to anticipate the worst. That way you're spared disappointments and, if things do go right, you have a pleasant surprise. So I told myself that it was impossible that I should be pregnant again right up to the moment when the doctor told me that the results of the test had proved positive.

'I was so happy, but again, I was not going to get over-excited. I told myself that this pregnancy, too, might well go wrong. I simply cancelled all my engagements, including, sadly, the Klemperer *Lohengrin* at Covent Garden and my longed-for *Carmen* under Buñuel. I engaged a nurse and settled down for a long, boring but worthwhile wait while nature did its job.'

On August 1, 1963, the woman who could never have a child of her own gave birth to a boy. He was christened Juan Enrique.

At last, then, a Victoria who was neither the remote and hard-working 'de los Angeles', nor the innocent, wistful caretaker's daughter 'Vittorina' was liberated. This Victoria was a mixture of the two. She was tough, practical, loving, committed and happy. She knew now where she was going and why.

Right from the beginning, Victoria had a nurse for her son so that, when she again took up her career, he would not be disorientated by her absence. The nurse had an excellent habit of singing—rather off key, or so Victoria thought—to the baby when she gave him his feed. Victoria also liked to sing to him. The only trouble was that, as soon as Victoria opened her mouth to sing, Juan Enrique screamed as though in agony. Victoria actually had to imitate the nurse's voice if he was to remain happy and peaceful. 'So much for his musical future!', she laughs.

When Juan Enrique was old enough to accompany her, Victoria paid an important call. She went back to the doctor who had advised her that she would never have children of her own. 'You remember you said that I could never have a baby?' she said. 'Well, look how wrong you were!'

Two months after his birth, Victoria was back before the public with a special concert at Amsterdam's Concertgebouw. At the end of the evening, she was presented with the Edison Prize in recognition of her outstanding recording achievements.

Recitals in Germany, Holland and England followed. She deliberately chose locations close enough to Barcelona for her to be able to fly back after only a day or two's absence from Juan Enrique. At Christmas, Victoria, José and Carmen, all now with families of their own, enjoyed a chaotic but happy few days together. 'Now for the first time I began to think of having proper holidays. I decided that I would try to take a month off every summer. That first year, we booked a villa on the coast and took my mother down there with us. I had never had a complete month off work, except during my pregnancy. I don't think that I could have stood the inactivity before, but now that I had Juan Enrique, it was marvellous. I remember thinking how sad it was that my father was not still alive. I'm sure that we could have even persuaded him to leave his precious university for a month and to come down with us. He'd have loved to play the proud grandfather. I felt closer to my mother than ever before. When my father was alive, she was always very retiring—very Spanish in taking second place to her husband all the time. Now I could enjoy long periods alone with her, like the summer season at Bayreuth and our holiday by the sea. I began to appreciate what a really nice person she was—in real terms, rather than simply as my mother. She never spoke ill of anybody and she was always anxious to help wherever she could. She was a great friend, and I had never really known it until then.'

Victoria returned to opera in September 1964, again at the Colón theatre in Buenos Aires. She sang the Countess in *The Marriage of Figaro*. When first she had sung the part, she had been an unmarried twenty-one-year-old and had had to rely on instinct for her interpretation of the role. Now, like the Countess, she was a mother. Now, too, like the Countess, she had more experience of life and realized that it held some bitter disappointments.

The noble serenity of the Countess sometimes seemed a mockery to Victoria. It was not easy to portray such a noble and serene character, especially when her real character was more like that of Butterfly: romantic, childlike, trusting. 'In life you have to learn that love on its own is not enough. You must bring infinite patience, intelligence and understanding to a marriage over the years.'

Victoria's marriage was very conventionally Spanish—just as her parents' had been. For all her international fame and reputation, Victoria's married role was that of her mother's, an obedient, patient and retiring wife to a husband who was, as her father had been, 'the boss'. Right from the very beginning of her singing days when her first fees had been handed over to her mother and father, Victoria had never touched the business side of her career. She would have found it impossible to do so now.

'Of course, everyone has their problems and must learn to overcome them. The trouble is that when you are a singer, problems like that inevitably affect your voice. A voice is not something that you can just take out of a music case before a concert. It is a part of you, and its very tone is always expressing something about you. If you are worried or unhappy, it is reflected in your performance.'

For all her problems, Victoria's career continued to gather momentum. In 1965, she made her recital debut in Vienna, toured France and Germany and made her operatic debut in Geneva, the scene of her first international triumph, in an uneven and garish production of *Faust*. She then flew to Japan for the Osaka festival. 'Unfortunately, I caught a cold on the way out, but I decided to go ahead with most of the concerts in Osaka and Tokyo nonetheless. I had learned how to control the voice and to make the most of it since the days of my Carnegie Hall debut. Anyhow, although I was nervous, the Japanese liked me and I must say that I liked them very much. It was fascinating to see the real Japan after all those years of playing *Butterfly*.'

Enrique, too, developed a great affection for the East and all things Eastern on this trip, and bought large numbers of fine pictures. He had decided to invest in property and had started to build a block of flats in the Avenida de la Victoria, an appropriately named and very exclusive boulevard in Barcelona. The top floor was to be their new home, and these Eastern works were to supply the prevalent *motif* in an apartment so large that it could house all the trophies acquired in their years of world travel. He bought well. Many of those paintings have since quadrupled in value.

'Enrique has always been a great collector of things,' says Victoria. 'He has a very famous collection of stamps, and he

138

has collected some fine sports cars over the years. I have never had the patience. A collector has to be a very dedicated sort of person, a very selective sort of person. I cannot criticise everything I see like that. It's the same with my music. I love *all* music. I don't just obsessively collect one special sort.

'I understood Enrique's insistence on moving to a bigger place, but really I was quite happy with the old house in the Calle Calvet. It was not too big, it was quite comfortable, it was home. Of course, I love good paintings, but I'd rather see them in museums and galleries. So much talent and work goes into a good work that it is a tragic waste to keep them at home. After only a short time, you stop looking at them.'

They had considerable problems bringing Enrique's acquisitions through customs on their return to Spain. At last, Enrique hit on a ruse, 'This is Victoria de los Angeles, the opera singer. You've heard of her? Yes? Good. Have you ever been to the opera? Good. Now, my wife's most famous role is that of a Japanese girl in *Madam Butterfly*. You've heard of that? Splendid. It's set in Japan, isn't it? And how exactly do you expect my wife to perform an opera set in Japan without Japanese props?'

Stunned, the customs men let the 'props' pass into Spain.

Hardly had the paintings been unwrapped, however, before they had to leave again, this time for a tour of Australia and New Zealand. Victoria gave a total of seventeen concerts in June and the first half of July. She was greeted with warmth and enthusiasm. Two newspapers complained that Christchurch, New Zealand had been left out of the itinerary. Victoria amended her schedule. 'I really enjoyed the tour', Victoria recalls, 'but I was still longing to get back home for my summer holiday with Juan Enrique and my mother. Enrique drove us down to the Catalan coast and we spent all of August there. It was lovely, but all too short. It only seemed a matter of days before Enrique was back with contracts to be signed and plans to be discussed for 1966. The highlights of the year were to be recitals and concerts in Scandinavia, Belgium, France, Switzerland and England, culminating in a concert at the Royal Festival Hall in the presence of the Queen.

'On occasions that year I had problems with my voice. Of course, they always had to crop up at the big, special concerts like the one for the Queen.'

Some of Victoria's admirers noticed that she had been having difficulties and wrote expressing concern. Their fears were allayed to some extent, however, by the release of her second recording of *La vida breve*, in which she had rarely been heard in better voice.

She was able to fulfil only two major opera bookings in the next few months. She played *Manon* at the Liceo and was given a generous 'welcome back' by the Barcelona public. Many who had first heard her singing this part in the 'forties observed that, although her middle register was as lovely and compelling as ever, she seemed to be having difficulties with her top notes.

Her next booking was at Dallas, where once she had hoped to sing *Carmen*. She had been invited there to sing Desdemona to Jon Vickers' Otello. Just before she left for America, she was told the news that she had been longing for. She was pregnant once again.

This, Dallas Opera's twelfth season, was particularly successful. The huge theatre was packed out for the performances of *Otello*, the first full houses there since Callas sang *Medea* in 1958. Victoria overcame most of her vocal problems for these performances and was rewarded by the plaudits of audiences and critics. She returned to Barcelona hoping for total peace and quiet as she awaited the new baby.

Total peace and quiet, however, proved impossible. The new home that Enrique had been building on the Avenida de la Victoria was now ready. They gave their old house on the Calle Calvet to Victoria's mother, and moved into the palatial new premises. 'Home' was now the top two storeys of a sleek, high-rise apartment block. It commanded magnificent views over the city and the port. For all her reservations about the size of the place, Victoria was happy to live high above the ground once more.

Again, Enrique had taken complete control of the layout and decor of their home. Victoria had no idea what to expect

140

when first she stepped into the lift and pressed the topmost button. 'I was right at the top of the huge building before I had even realised that the lift had started to move. I stepped out and climbed a small staircase and found myself up on the roof. There was a swimming pool there, and a roof garden with trees and shrubs already planted. Below was the living area, including several living rooms, a music room, a series of bedrooms, all with bathroom *en suite*, a large kitchen and the staff quarters. Everything had a cool sheen to it.'

The style was, in fact, not unlike that of the very best modern international hotels. Once Victoria's piano and her countless souvenirs were installed, however, the cool, polished elegance began to be invested with the qualities of a home.

Within a very short time, the various rooms reflected their owners' different personalities and interests. Enrique's bathroom was a model of gleaming, hygienic order while Victoria's was, to put it mildly, chaos. Bottles and brushes and pictures and clothes piled up around the exercise-cycle which she deliberately set up in the centre of the room as a constant reminder of the perils of overweight. Enrique had his hi-fi equipment installed in a whole series of concealing cabinets and cupboards and panels in one large living room. Victoria, on the other hand, assembled all her photographs, trophies and souvenirs in an apparently haphazard way around her beloved Steck. A second piano stood in the main living room.

A wide balcony ran around the whole apartment so that you could slide back the smoked glass doors and stroll out for a 180-degree view of the city. Outside the main bedroom, a fountain had been installed because Victoria had always loved the sight and sound of running water. The trees in the roof garden soon created problems. 'One day I came down after having spent a few hours sitting amongst them to find a huge crack in the ceiling of the room below. By the time that we got someone around to investigate, several more splits had appeared, and I thought the whole flat was going to fall apart. I wasn't that far wrong. They said that the trees would have

141

to be uprooted immediately, or else they would destroy the building.

'I don't know,' she sighs. 'I suppose that Enrique did all this for me or, at least, for what he thought of as the star—Victoria de los Angeles—and I should be grateful, but I really had been quite content with our old home. It was at least a real home. My only pipe dream is of a chalet up in the mountains with a big log fire and lots of books. That's what I'd have asked for if I had been consulted. Enrique thought that Victoria de los Angeles should have a star's house, an exhibition house. Maybe she should, but it's not what Victoria wants or ever wanted.'

The fates were still not prepared to forgive Victoria for the natural talent which had transformed her from caretaker's daughter to international star. Her pregnancy was normal. The birth was without difficulties. The child was retarded.

'When Alejandro was born', Victoria remembers, 'everybody except me knew that he had Down's syndrome. I had been very disappointed when an earlier pregnancy had been terminated after one month, and I think nobody wanted me to be worried. But I believe it really was a mistake for me not to have known. It would have been much better for me to be prepared. I was a much stronger person than they took me for. After Alejandro's birth, he was kept under observation for twenty-four hours and then he was shown to me. I said to Enrique, "Why did you not tell me? Why did you keep it a secret?" And I took the little boy into my arms with such love.

'As a baby he was terribly soft. The muscles of little boys like him don't work well, and so they are rubbery and floppy. Their hands flop down, their arms flop down. You have to be patient because it takes a very long time for them to develop. And gradually, when they begin to express themselves with some movement, you fully realise how sweet they are. There is a whole world of expression in their faces. My feeling was that it was a blessing in my house. I loved him with a special tenderness because he was handicapped.'

Victoria left Alejandro for the first time three months after his birth. She toured South Africa in May, 1968. Once again,

142

her career, on which her family, the new home and the Magriña investments all depended, had to keep going, and she had to learn not to worry about her sons while she was away. She had appointed the best nurses available to take care of them, and she knew that unnecessary anxiety would help neither her singing nor her children. 'I tried to organise my career so that I could be away for short periods of ten or fifteen days and then be home and be a good mother until it was time to fly off again for a few days.'

For all her resolve not to worry, Victoria did not want to be too far from baby Alejandro in the first months of his life, even for the shortest periods. While he was still small, therefore, she attempted to restrict her appearances to France and Great Britain, and flew back as soon as the concerts were over.

By summer of 1969, Juan Enrique was already six, and Victoria could sometimes take him with her. He provided welcome company. He was particularly fascinated by recording sessions. Victoria has an especially charming photograph of her elder son in short trousers, gazing through the plate glass of the studio at his mother who is singing into the microphone.

Victoria decided not to undertake any operatic engagements outside Spain in 1969. She first sang the role of Charlotte in *Werther* in Madrid that year. 'I had already recorded it before ever I sang it on stage. It was a pity that it had to be that way round. It's always better if you can play the role first and really understand the character before you make a recording.

'Charlotte was very different from the other heroines that I had played. Whereas all my other roles were those of women who perished, or, at least, suffered for the love of their men, Charlotte reverses the roles. It's the man that dies for her. I cannot say that I rubbed my hands together with glee and thought, "At last, a man has died for me!" but I did feel that this stronger, more resilient role reflected a change in me as well. I had become a fighter. I never believed in making a lot of noise about the struggles of life, but I had had my fair share over the last few years. At the beginning of my career, everything just happened. I always tried to sing as best as I could, but otherwise I did not have to struggle to make my name. By 1970, it was not so easy. I had acquired many new responsibilities and many new problems. With them, though, had come the strength—perhaps some would say the ferocity—to take those responsibilities, to solve those problems. I was not afraid. I really thought that nothing was impossible, so long as I was prepared to get my priorities right and to sacrifice one thing in order to obtain another. I had never had to do that before, but once I had children, I was forced to fight as I had never fought before. In the end, it was good that I did, because, if you do not fight, you die!'

14

'Maybe it seems that Enrique is conspicuous by his absence in the story of my life, but it should not really be so. He has always been with me, and I do want to say how very grateful I am to him for everything that he has done—the care that he has taken, the protection that he has given me.'

Enrique had been Victoria's manager since they were married in 1948. He had travelled everywhere with her, and they had come a long, long way together since their first American tour when Victoria had been unknown, and they had lost their luggage on Grand Central Station and ended up penniless in Cuba. Now, through virtually non-stop work and travel, they had a magnificent home in which to bring up their two children, there was not a major opera house in the world in which Victoria had not performed, nor a music-lover who had not at least one of her many records.

Now Enrique's energy and enthusiasm began to flag. After so many years of negotiating fees, overseeing publicity, setting up the lighting for concerts and waiting in the wings with a glass of water at Victoria's every performance, he sometimes longed to stay at home in Barcelona with his friends and to tend the many business interests which had grown up over the years.

Many of Victoria's friends and associates, such as Gerald Moore and David Bicknell of EMI, remained bemused at the couple's continued success, for, although Enrique employed a secretary, they have never known him to answer a single letter. 'It's as though her career had been promoted and administered in a world of unending *mañanas*.' Yet for all his apparent inefficiency, Enrique somehow contrived to organise a busy and successful career for twenty-two years.

If Enrique was no longer so keen, Victoria's enthusiasm seemed unabated as the 'seventies began. She was increasingly abandoning the world of opera and concentrating on her recital career; but, although she had finally put the Mimìs, Manons and Butterflies behind her, she felt that she would still leap at the chance to play Carmen.

*   *   *

On November 20, 1975, General Franco died and King Juan Carlos assumed power. The new regime introduced many liberal policies. One of the most significant reforms was the introduction of greater independence and civil rights for Spanish women. Victoria had never been a liberated woman. She does not like to think of herself as such now. But she increasingly understood the folly of the traditional attitude of Spanish wives to their menfolk. Listening to the new generation of Spanish women, she decided to be responsible henceforth for her own life and that of her children.

Victoria's progress around the world continued, therefore, but she became a new Victoria. She had gone on a crash slimming course and had also become a more vivacious person, less restrained by the bonds of shyness which had inhibited her for so long. Her concert notes for the 'seventies show that she appeared in the Soviet Union, Hungary, Italy, Spain, France, Great Britain, Central and South America and Scandinavia. She also made four coast-to-coast tours of the United States. Although her personality and artistry remained unchanged, she was careful to adjust her repertoire to her voice and if things went wrong, sometimes to heal her voice with exercises until she had overcome the difficulty.

Sometimes, a cold or an allergy caused terrible difficulties and at times she felt that she would never sing well again. These were deeply depressing periods, and Victoria would spend weeks in solitary despair, before recovering her optimism and her powers.

Once, after an exhausting tour of Great Britain which left her with a chest cold, Victoria relied on her experience and her personality rather than cancel the last concert of the tour at the Royal Festival Hall. At the end of the evening, two friends from Paris came backstage and told her, 'We just had to come and see you. We thought you were *awful*.' With no ill-humour, they proceeded to catalogue the disasters of the evening. At last Victoria looked up, smiling, 'Look, I don't mind your saying that to me, but please, please, make it a principle never to say such things to anyone when they have just finished a performance. Any performer lays himself wide open on stage. He throws down all his defences. When he comes offstage, he is still like a snail without a shell. If you ever spoke to a young performer or anyone less self-critical than I as you have just spoken to me, you could destroy his confidence for a very long time—perhaps, even, forever.'

Werther was Victoria's last recorded opera, but her name was still prominent in the lists of best-selling classical recording artists by reason of a series of song albums and the reissue of some of the earlier mono records now reprocessed for stereo reproduction. It was now clear that some of these reissues, notably the Beecham *La Bohème* and *Carmen* and the Rome recordings of *Simon Boccanegra* and *Trittico* with Gobbi were not just good specimens of the period but definitive classics.

Of the song albums, in which Victoria recorded much of her extensive repertoire, perhaps the most interesting was the live recording made at Hunter College, New York, on the twenty-fifth anniversary of the death of Manuel de Falla, November 13, 1971. She was accompanied by Alicia de Larrocha at the piano. Larrocha had also been born and brought up in Barcelona. What the New York audience did not know, however, was that this marked the renewal of a collaboration which had started thirty-two years earlier, when Victoria, then a first-year student at the Barcelona Conservatorio, had made a practice record at the Odeon studios in Madrid. The promising young pianist chosen to accompany her had been Alicia de Larrocha.

Victoria disliked the business of making records in the studio. She missed the give and take of interaction with an audience. Her 'Songs of the Auvergne' album proved so popular that she had to record a second selection. As she steeled herself to enter the studio, she said to herself, 'Everyone tells me that millions of people like these records. I just wish that a couple of hundred of them could be here!'

Another memorable performance of these years was a concert version of the little opera which had always been associated with Victoria since she recorded it for the B.B.C. in 1948, *La vida breve*. She sang it at the Royal Albert Hall in April 1973. 'I had sung it at festivals—Granada, the Holland Festival, Edinburgh—with the dance element sometimes overshadowing and spoiling the effect of the singing. Really I had come to prefer performing it on radio or for record. But there was not that problem at the Albert Hall in a concert version though the size of the hall was not ideal for it. I performed it only three times more after that. I was booked to do four performances at the Savoy theatre, Boston, 1979. A heavy cold forced me to cancel the last. I knew that I had sung Salud for the last time.'

In November 1978, the opportunity to play Carmen on

148

stage at last arose. She was asked to play Bizet's heroine at the Newark Festival with the New Jersey State Opera. 'The main reason that I had always wanted to play Carmen was that she is so very Spanish. She moves her hands in a Spanish way. She sings in a Spanish way. I wanted to present that Spanish character in theatrical terms, as I had presented so many other aspects of my character and upbringing in theatrical terms. I wanted to be able to go on stage with those Spanish costumes, to play the castanets, to sing her vivacious music, to put across all the coquetry of a woman of Spain. If I had simply wanted to portray a woman in love, I could have stuck with Butterfly, who, after all, conceives of love in much the same romantic, absolutist way as I. But just because I am a romantic, it does not mean that there is not in me a degree of earthiness. It is not something that you should show. It is something kept in reserve, but it is there, it is always there, and especially perhaps in Spanish women. Then, too, there is the staging of *Carmen*—the problem of capturing the Spanish colours, the *feel* of Spain. My greatest ambition in opera had long been to present the definitive Spanish *Carmen*. It would take a wonderful stage director, a first-class designer, really imaginative lighting. . . . I did not have these when at last I came to play Carmen, so I don't really feel that I've ever played the part on stage.'

She did, however, demonstrate to New Jersey audiences just what a Carmen she could have been. *Opera* magazine wrote, 'Anyone who feels that style and elegance have disappeared from the operatic stage should have been in New Jersey on November 4. Carmen is no lady. But neither is she the bosom-heaving, hip-swinging slut portrayed by most interpreters of the role. Los Angeles created a sleek, sensual gypsy, a playful but proud woman who embraced love flirtatiously and faced her tragic fate with difficulty . . . although her voice has lost some of its velvet and lacks fullness on top and intensity of tone for the climactic phrases, she projected the elegant sensuality of Bizet's music and conveyed the ironic humour and matchless charm of Meilhac and Halévy's text. . . . I do not remember los Angeles as much of an actress, but her Carmen was an acting triumph. Radiating charm and irresistible allure, she looked very beautiful in a succession of handsome costumes whose colour and cut mirrored Carmen's transition from carefree enchantress to fate-driven woman. I shall not soon forget the magnetic spell she cast in the first entrance or the beguiling grace with which she bewitched José. Like all great artists, los Angeles knows the value of stillness. In the card scene, she projected dark intensity, standing motionless, her exquisite pale features framed in the dusky light. She was a radiant, unforgettable Carmen.'

If Webster at Covent Garden or Bing at the Metropolitan had seen what Buñuel saw, it is impossible to resist the thought that she might have found a role as central to her art as Scarpia was to Gobbi or Violetta to Callas. When Victoria at last brought her stage interpretation to the New York City Opera a year later, a combination of strikes and backstage problems prevented rehearsals. After just one performance, the rest were cancelled.

She wished farewell to two last opera roles in the 'seventies. The first was Charlotte in *Werther*, which she performed as a special favour for director Margherita Wallmann. Obratsova, who had been billed to sing the role at the Colón, was indisposed, and Wallmann telephoned to ask if Victoria could help out and stand in at short notice. That Victoria agreed to do so reflects the high esteem in which she held Wallmann. 'Of all the many opera directors with whom I have worked over the years, Wallmann is the one that I most admire and always felt most relaxed with.' For the many de los Angeles fans who remembered her from the days of her first South American tours in the 'fifties and who packed out the theatre, it was sad that the emergency prevented her from doing herself justice. Some, who cherished memories of *Butterfly* and *Bohème*, and did not know she was struggling to overcome a cold, suggested that she should leave the opera stage for good and concentrate instead on her recitals. For Victoria, the recital hall continued to be what it always had been even in her years at the Metropolitan—the most satisfying place for performing her music.

She accepted, however, an invitation to sing Mélisande in Madrid in 1980. She had no intention of making a 'farewell performance'. *Prima donnas'* farewells are, after all, a standing joke. But Mélisande is a role which taxes a singer's musicianship more than her vocal powers. In terms of musicianship and experience, Victoria had been growing every year even as her voice grew weaker. Now she was peerless, and the Madrid audience acknowledged the fact at this performance, her first in Europe of one of her most famous roles.

Her triumph was all the more remarkable because it occurred at a time of intense private pain. Alejandro simply seemed to be fading away. No one knew the cause, but with each day he grew paler and weaker and his eyes grew wilder. For a while, Victoria had sent him to a day school for backward children. She had found, however, that he responded better to the company of people who were not handicapped. She next changed schools and sought a suitable private tutor. Then suddenly, as he passed into adolescence, it became clear that he was very sick indeed.

Doctors searched for any trace of leukaemia or other blood disorders. They found nothing. Victoria took him away for a holiday in the Montseny in the hope that the mountain air might at least give him strength to fight. He perked up a little, but it did not reverse the process of degeneration.

At last, Victoria sent him to a private clinic in Madrid. Every test from brain scans to lumbar punctures was made. He just lay there, pale, scared and silent. Victoria slept by his hospital bed every night, willing him to hold on, 'Just one more night. Please. Hold on just one more night. . . .'

And then the tide turned, and it was over. Mélisande was a great success, and on one of her numerous visits to the hospital Victoria was informed that there had been an improvement in Alejandro's condition. He went on improving. In a few weeks, he was back home with a stomach swollen like a balloon. Victoria had to buy him a complete new wardrobe of clothes.

The passage of the months brought colour to his cheeks, and he began to put on weight. Soon Victoria started to teach him to read and resumed the quest for a tutor. 'The strain of worry

151

had exhausted me', Victoria remembers, 'but sometimes I couldn't sleep and just had to creep along to his room to look at him. I couldn't believe that he was still there, or that he wasn't going to be snatched away from me. But it was all right. We'd won. He would live.'

It had been discovered that Alejandro's digestive system could not assimilate gluten. 'If only we had known, we would have put him on this diet long ago, because without it he is unable to digest his food and for that reason he grew slowly. Now he seems to have grown ten years in one. He is learning the letters of the alphabet and is a very willing pupil. We have put him in a small private class for other children who live nearby, and he is making enormous progress.' Alejandro, who always embraces visitors and repeats at the top of his voice their words of greeting, is just becoming strong enough to lift some of them off their feet in his affectionate bear hugs.

Probably the most far-reaching event for Victoria in the 1970s was the illness and death of her mother at the beginning of the decade.

'My mother became very ill', Victoria remembers, 'in the autumn of 1970. She had a brain haemorrhage, which left her with a twitch on her right side. Then gradually she became paralysed. The doctors told me that she was going to die and suggested that we put her into a clinic. I refused because I wanted to nurse her myself, and they brought her up to my home.

'Towards the end she did not recognise me very well. I often sang to her, and sometimes when I finished she said, "Very good. But my daughter, Victoria, sings better than you." She was given cortisone treatment and that kept her alive for three-and-a-half months. I never left her. I saw to the pre-scriptions, the pills, the injections, the massages. For those three-and-a-half months my whole life was spent either in her bedroom or in the kitchen cooking for her and nursing her.

'When she died and we buried her one grey February day, I suddenly realised that I had never really got to know her until after my father died. Only then had she come to life for me as a person in her own right. I expected my father's death

152

(*Above*) Recording *Faust* in Paris with
Boris Christoff, Nicolai Gedda and Rita
Gorr

(*Right*) Victoria with Thomas
Beecham, her conductor for two
all-time great recordings—*La Bohème*
in America and *Carmen* in Paris

(*Opposite top*) Victoria at EMI's studios in Barcelona where she was formally made the studio's 'godmother'

(*Opposite bottom*) Recording *Cavalleria Rusticana* with Franco Corelli in 1963

(*Above*) At the formal opening of the new EMI studios in Barcelona

(*Above*) Victoria with Gerald Moore, her accompanist in recitals all over the world

(*Opposite bottom*) When Victoria sang Mélisande for the last time in Madrid in 1980 her elder son Juan Enrique came along to do the dressing room honours

At the Aldeburgh Festival 1975: signing autographs and (*left*) with accompanist Miguel Zanetti

(*Above*) At London's Duke of York's
Theatre in 1980 Glenda Jackson
presents Victoria with a Golden Disc
from EMI in recognition of her 30 years
of recording with the company

(*Opposite*) At home in Spain in the
early 1970s

would have a great effect on me, but surprisingly my mother's death had a much bigger one. After she died I began to open up as a person. Before, for example, if somebody wanted me to sign my autograph I did so without comment. But from time to time onwards I began to talk to people, to find out about them and about their lives. I began to have more confidence in myself. When I went back to England and America in the 1970s on recital tours, people who had known me sing at the beginning of my career said, "Victoria, you are another person!"

'When my mother was very sick, I got to know Father Leon, who came to pray with her and to perform the last rites. He now comes to see me regularly and we chat. I had never liked the confessional in church and always preferred to confess alone with God.

15

'I never wanted to make a recording in my life. To do so was always torture to me. I am by nature a perfectionist, and I never believe that what I am doing is good enough. So when I was planning ahead a schedule of opera and concerts and was told, "No, you must keep this period free for recording", I hated the thought that I had to do it. I really did! And I *never* listen to my own recordings.'

Despite her hatred of the recording studio—even, perhaps, because of it—Victoria de los Angeles is generally considered to be one of the most successful recording artists of the post-war years, and therefore of all time. The two opera recordings that she made with Beecham, *Carmen* in Paris and *La Bohème* in the United States, are now regarded as classics. No collection of opera recordings would be considered complete, too, without the Monteux *Manon* and one of the two *Butterfly*s—that she recorded with di Stefano in Rome or that with Björling. Her song albums are remarkable in that they contain not only the commonly performed works from the French, Italian, English and German recital repertoire but also many Spanish and Catalan songs for whose current fame she and she alone is responsible. Add to the list her best-selling *Homage to Gerald Moore*, an exuberant live performance by Victoria, Schwarzkopf, Fischer-Dieskau and, of course, the great accompanist himself, and you have a catalogue so rich and so varied that it is hard to believe that they spring from unhappiness.

The facts of the de los Angeles recording career were related to the public at the Duke of York's theatre in London on a Sunday evening in May, 1980. E.M.I. asked Glenda Jackson to present Victoria with a special golden disc to mark thirty years of exclusive performance on the H.M.V., E.M.I. and Angel labels. In that time, she had made twenty-one complete opera recordings. Four had been recorded twice. E.M.I. never release sales figures, but a figure 'well in excess of five million' long-playing records was mentioned.

It is a commonplace among carpers that Caruso's reputation depends rather on the fact that he was the resident tenor at La Scala at the time of the commercial development of phonographic records than upon his abilities. However that may be, it is unquestionable that Caruso was fortunate. Like many of those who attain greatness, he was in the right place at the right time. The same is true of Victoria. She established herself as a bright new talent and as an E.M.I. performer in the late 'forties and 'fifties, the last days of 78 rpm records. You may yet find one of these records; two sections of *La vida breve,* a few Gounod, Massenet, Mozart and Wagner arias, some few Spanish songs. But Victoria reached the height of her powers and her fame at the same time as reasonably-priced 33 rpm long-playing records were coming onto the market.

It is hard to conceive of a world in which records could not be bought, in which the nearest thing to musical excellence available to the average music-lover was a concert at the town hall or an occasional broadcast on the wireless. We are besieged now with records and all the cults attendant upon their sales. Yet Victoria was at the top of her trade at a time when all that was just beginning. What Frank Sinatra or Elvis Presley were to the new music (in terms of the booming record industry), Victoria and her contemporaries were to the classical market.

'In my childhood—throughout my childhood, gramophones were status symbols', she recalls. 'We never had records at home. Nowadays, a stereo system is a standard item of furniture. You can hear great singers and great orchestras at the push of a button. I didn't even really know what opera was until I went to the Conservatorio. There was one neighbour, I remember, who had a wind-up cabinet machine of which he was immensely proud. But it shows how rare they were in those days when I tell you that he used to invite people round specially to listen to pasodobles on it.

'During the civil war, of course, books and records were looted. I vaguely remember our neighbour asking us round to listen to a couple of Caruso and Tetrazzini records which had been stolen and somehow found their way to him. It was a miracle that they survived without being broken. I know that I thought they were much more interesting than the paso-dobles had been, but I never had any ambition to be a singer then—how could I? I didn't really know what a singer was—and it was no more than a passing interest. Years later, *Ars Musicae* presented me with one of those little black wind-up things with steel needles so that I could play the records that we had made.'

The situation was largely unchanged by the time that Victoria started her own international recording career in 1948. True, the records were now made on tape and later transferred to those heavy and frangible wax discs rather than being recorded direct on wax. True, too, richer countries than Spain now boasted large record sales amongst the middle classes, but, with the coming of the long-playing record, when Victoria had made only twenty-five records, music reached the masses for the first time.

Those twenty-five records—all, now, incidentally, collectors' items—may sound like a prodigious output for a young singer at the beginning of her career. The figure can be put into proportion by the fact that the previous classic *Madam Butterfly* by Toti del Monte, with which Victoria's 1955 recording was favourably compared, occupied the surface of sixteen records. You had to get up thirty-two times in order to change the record when it was first issued. Victoria's recording, on the other hand, could be heard on a three-record set. No wonder then that the old 78s were being deleted, and every great work had to be recorded again by the leading performers of the day.

'Yes, it was a golden age in that there was such a huge demand for our services, but also in that there were technicians who really knew what your voice should sound like and how to reproduce it. The people in charge cared about the artistic, and not merely the business side of things. That was marvellous. The problem for me was that I missed the audience, that special contact which you get with an audience and which makes the difference between a great and a moderate performance. With a good audience, I find that I can do things that I really never believed to be possible. When all you've got to sing to is a microphone, there's none of that human warmth! When I sing in an opera house or a concert hall, I have an intuitive feeling about the audience's response. That is very important. I gain confidence from them. I find that I can do things for them that I really didn't believe would be possible. But in a recording studio you really have to forget about that altogether.

'I really don't think that I'd have managed at all in those early years had it not been for David Bicknell at E.M.I—or H.M.V., as it then was. He was so much more than just a businessman. He had been with the company since the 'twenties and knew the whole business inside out, but from the artist's point of view as well as that of the producers and distributors. I trusted him absolutely. I could say to him, "Look, I don't feel well today. I can't do it as it should be done," and he would give me a day off, I would rest, and then I'd come back the next day full of life. He not only knew more about recording techniques than anyone around at the time, he also understood artists. He knew that an unhappy singer would make a bad record. In turn, he trusted me. That enabled me to relax and do my best work.'

That Bicknell's patient approach paid off is demonstrated by the manner in which the now legendary Monteux/de los

158

Angeles *Manon* was recorded. For some days, the rest of the cast worked without Victoria. At length, the old Swiss maestro approached Bicknell and demanded that Victoria should join them. Still Victoria delayed. Bicknell at once supported her and appeased Monteux. At the eleventh hour, Victoria found her confidence and completed the whole recording in an astonishing three sessions crammed into one day. Monteux, by then in his mid-eighties, had to cat-nap between sessions. The hall of the Palais de la Mutualité therefore was plunged into darkness from time to time while the conductor, on a made-up bed, restored his strength in sleep.

'It is extraordinary how someone else, whether it be an audience or someone like David Bicknell or Gerald Moore, can give you confidence to do things you could never otherwise do,' says Victoria. 'During that recording, I had got as far as the Cours-la-Reine scene at the beginning of Act III, and I had decided not to sing the top D. Manon, you know, is singing provocatively of the gay life she now leads. I did not have that note in my range, and I did not want to risk spoiling everything by trying for it. Massenet, after all, had only written it in to please Marie Heilbronn, who created the role at the Opéra Comique. The lower G does just as well.

'We were just about to do the scene when the tenor Legay, who was singing des Grieux, said in passing, "Of course, you'll be doing the top D?"

"Of course she will," said Enrique.

"I couldn't possibly," I told them.

"But it's become a tradition in France," Legay insisted. "You must do it."

"But I've never sung a top D!"

"All the more reason to try now."

'The leader of the orchestra was no fool. He just touched the D on his highest string. He must have known that it would act as a spur to my vanity. "All right", I said, "I'll try."

'And I reached it! I urged it out very gently and pianissimo, then let it swell and sparkle for a moment. Then it faded away.

159

'Legay was like a dog with two tails. "You have a top D like that," he said, "and you want to keep it to yourself? It's criminal!"

'I always had it. I just did not sing it in public.'

The bulk of Victoria's recordings of complete operas were made either at the Opera House in Rome or at the Salle Wagram in Paris, depending on the language demanded of the supporting cast. London's Abbey Road studios were used for the song albums, save in the case of Spanish songs which were usually recorded in Barcelona or Madrid. 'Paris' Salle Wagram and the Rome Opera House were both good places to work. Both had first-rate acoustics for the purpose. Oh, it was a wonderful feeling to be on that stage in Rome. I could almost forget that I was recording as I stood in an Italian opera house singing Italian libretti. That gave me the sort of boost that I need to sing well. On the other hand, I'm afraid that I found the Abbey Road studios rather sad, hygienic and melancholy. When I sang the songs that I usually sing in recitals, I missed my audience more than ever. Even the walls of a place, you see, can be alive and stimulating or dead and depressing. Without an orchestra, with just an accompanist, I missed an audience even more.'

Once, in Rome for the recording of *Butterfly*, Victoria, Jussi Björling and David Bicknell lunched in a restaurant in order to discuss further operas that they might record together. They separated and, when Victoria and Bicknell turned up at the Opera House for the afternoon session, they found that Björling was not there. The stage doorkeeper reported that he had turned up, but had left suddenly in order to retrieve some vital pills that he had left in his hotel.

They found the possessor of 'the greatest tenor voice God ever made' sprawled across the bed in his hotel room. Still only forty-nine, he had had a heart attack. He was still able to speak, 'I'm sorry, I'll be back in a fortnight.' He was, and the recording was safely completed. Only a couple of months later, in September, 1960, he suffered a further, fatal attack.

'It's extraordinary how recording sessions vary,' says Victo-

160

ria. 'The *Bohème*, for instance, was completed in the space of a few days in America. We all just happened to be free for a short period, so we got together and did it. Normally, however, you have to sing for a minimum of three hours a day for something between ten and sixteen days. Often, you begin in the morning and don't go home till late at night, just to save money on studio time. It's ridiculous. The voice gets tired, just like any other part of you. You come to a big dramatic moment after days of singing and you look for the wonderful, natural, relaxed sound that you know you owe to the scene. It's just not there any more. It's terrifying to think that people are going to sit down and listen, expecting you to sing as you would in a normal evening's performance. It's vital that you should retain your freshness and enthusiasm for every scene. That's why I hate the whole business so much. The public can play a record again and again. Above all else, you just want it to be perfect. But you rarely have the chance to record it again and do it better.'

'When David Bicknell retired at the beginning of the 'seventies, all I heard was money, money, money. You weren't treated like an artist any more, just one cog among many in a money-machine. Everything good cost too much. You couldn't do this and you couldn't do that. The budget wouldn't stand it. It's impossible to do good work like that.

'The introduction of stereo meant that I was asked to repeat the roles that I had done before in mono—a new Manon for example. I even started to prepare a second *Bohème*. But I refused finally because I did not think that I could do them so well. It was not that I thought what I had done was so wonderful—only that I could not have done them any better.'

In 1958, Victoria was in Paris to record *Carmen*. Sir Thomas Beecham was to conduct. The auguries, certainly, were good. Their recording of *La Bohème* had been acclaimed throughout the world. For years, Victoria had wanted to play the part of Carmen instead of the surprisingly sweet Micaela, but she had been condemned on stage merely to sing the minor role. Now was her chance to prove that she could play the role.

She had rehearsed it at length in her studio. She arrived in Paris and took every care to ensure that she would be in ideal condition to give a top-class performance. She rested her voice, took plenty of exercise and slept a lot. She turned up for the first session feeling strong and confident. 'Of course it is better to have performed a work on stage before you record it, but I knew that I could sing Carmen even more surely than I had known that I could do *Butterfly*.

'As soon as we started to record, I realised there were problems with microphone adjustments and background noise. At any recording session, you expect to repeat sections for the sound engineers when this happens. After 15 days none of the singers had made *any* repeats. The engineers kept saying everything was just fine. In fact, I think they were worried that if they delayed Beecham, he would walk out. Everyone was a little in awe of him.

'Sir Thomas, of course, knew nothing of this. He and the orchestra worked in a different part of the studio, relying on the engineers' signals to stop and start. No one had approached him about the fact that the singers were upset, so the recording continued.'

Finally, prompted by the other singers, Victoria went to the producer. 'We were to record the '*Habanera*' and '*Seguidilla*' the next Saturday, and I wanted to make sure that, if things were not done correctly, I would be allowed to repeat. If not, I would leave.'

Saturday arrived. 'After the first effort, I asked to record the '*Habanera*' again. The engineers said, "No, no, it's wonderful. Let's go on to the '*Seguidilla*'." I was furious. I slapped down my score, left the studio and went back to my hotel. I decided to go home.'

David Bicknell was immediately called to Paris to smooth things over. He found Victoria at her hotel, packed and ready to leave for the airport. After listening to her side of the story, he went on to the studio. Beecham was there, still unaware that there was trouble. When Bicknell walked through the door, he merely said in offended tones: 'Ah, David. Perhaps you can tell me. Where *has* my Carmen gone?'

162

'At this moment,' Bicknell wearily replied, 'she is landing in Barcelona.'

The recording was suspended. Beecham flew to South America and, by chance, conducted *Carmen* at the Colón theatre in Buenos Aires. Bicknell now had to set about organising a set of dates for a Paris recording, when both Beecham and Victoria would be available, and willing, to try again. The dates were agreed, but only on assurances from Bicknell that he would be present throughout the sessions, and that any work done would be re-recorded if necessary.

The recording was completed in June, 1958. It won an award and an ecstatic press. In the February 1960 edition of *The Gramophone*, Philip Hope-Wallace began his notice: 'I send up a loud Olé. This *Carmen* wipes the floor with any other complete version I know, including the old 78s.'

Eight new complete opera recordings followed *Carmen* as well as recorded song recitals and two sacred works—the Fauré *Requiem* and the Berlioz *L'Enfance du Christ*. The 1960s rolled by and Victoria's most popular opera recordings—*Butterfly, Carmen* and *Manon*—appeared in one-record highlight editions. Few of those collecting her records would have guessed that with 20 years' experience behind her Victoria was still nervous of entering a studio.

'One of the most worrying things is that as recording becomes more sophisticated, you cannot be sure the sound engineer and his team will reproduce the actual sound of your voice. In the 1950s when I began, the engineers really knew and understood a singer's voice. They would never allow sounds to appear on a recording that were not your own. But later, when stereo began and I finished a recording I went to hear it played back, and sometimes I had to say, "Look, there is somebody else's voice here. Can you change that, please, so it is *my* voice."

'They adjusted the buttons,' Victoria goes on. 'They turned up the treble and turned down the bass to try to get it right. So I realised you couldn't be sure any more that you were going to hear your own voice. In spite of technical developments, none of the Jussi Björling recordings give you the true

163

sound of his voice. It was a far, far more beautiful voice than you can hear on the recordings he left.

'Another point is that even modern recordings are not at all fair in the reproduction of the *proportion* of voices. If you go to a live performance of an opera of, say, four lead voices, they will certainly not always be of the same size. One is almost certainly much bigger than the others. But on a recording, they all *sound* the same. It is a pity that a really warm and lustrous voice is made to sound just like any other voice. So I don't think you can just sit back and say how wonderful recordings now are. They must try to be even better. . . .'

The fact remains that one of the consequences of the LP revolution is a much wider audience for opera than there used to be. And this wider public will be served by a new generation of artists, some of whom will certainly consult the recordings Victoria has made of the Italian and French repertoire. But Victoria is not really in favour of this method of learning.

'Perhaps they should listen just once because they need to know—and then no more. If you admire a certain artist— good. If you admire di Stefano—good. If you admire Callas, Sutherland or even Victoria—good. But you should not sing *like* them. You should sing like yourself. If you listen to other singers, you risk copying them; and if you copy them and you are a talented young artist, you risk losing the possibility of finding a new way of singing from your imagination.

'When I sang *La Bohème* for the first time, I had never in my life heard anybody else sing it. This was true of the other roles—*Butterfly, Traviata, Manon*—never in my life had I heard anybody else sing them. I do sincerely believe that the interpretation must come from your own imagination, perhaps touched by the inspiration a live public gives you. In spite of all that has happened in recording since the 1940s, there is no pleasure like the pleasure of singing before a live public.'

Postscript

'You are very brave. I don't sing any more—not even at home.' The speaker was Renata Tebaldi. All too soon, the 1950s had become the 1980s, and Tebaldi had retired. But Victoria still maintained a busy recital schedule and it was on the Italian leg of one of these that she suddenly decided to phone Tebaldi at her home in the north of Italy at the start of the 1980s. Her reward was an affectionate greeting and the gravely spoken words, '*Sei molto coraggiosa, molto coraggiosa.*'

They did not discuss when Victoria might give up singing. 'I do not plan for it,' says Victoria quite simply. Nevertheless, as the 1970s have given way to the 1980s, the de los Angeles career has developed intriguing contrasts. On the one hand, it has broken some fresh ground. On the other, there has been some gentle rounding off of what has gone before. In 1979 Victoria went to Russia for the first time. But a year later she was back in London at the Wigmore Hall and in New York at the Carnegie Hall giving Thirtieth Anniversary Recitals of her sensational debuts on both platforms three decades before.

'Of course it is always good to be back in England and America,' says Victoria, 'but it was more exciting to be setting

165

off to Russia for the first time. Obviously, I would have been much more pleased with myself if I had managed to get to Russia much sooner—before it had begun to open out, to be there when there was still no cultural exchange so that one was being a pioneer. But even today they are still not used to overseas visitors and have very few singers and dancers from outside. They are a far less sophisticated audience than you find in the West with a result that you experience a higher degree of curiosity from the audiences—a more intense expectation. What I felt about them was a sense of purity—it was a very tender experience for me. As time goes by they are bound to lose their innocence. It makes me feel that I must hurry back to them before they become spoiled!'

In Russia and back on more familiar territory in the West Victoria began to be asked the same question. 'Why don't you also give Master Classes like so many of your colleagues? You could give such wonderful lessons on the singing of the traditional songs of Spain,' people said. 'In opera you could teach up-and-coming artists how to sing Mimì, Butterfly and Manon,' they usually added. Victoria's reply has always been gentle but firm:

'I prefer to help singers privately.' She explains, 'I do not think you should put yourself on show like that. Since I myself never learned by imitating other singers when I was young, I do not think it right for a younger singer to try to copy me now. Of course, if a young artist writes and asks to see me about a particular problem, then I really do enjoy trying to help that artist find his own—not my—solution. But preferably in private—not before the public.'

So, as the 1980s get underway, Victoria's life follows the broad pattern that was established when she began to have her own family in the 1960s. Short bursts of activity in Europe or America are followed by a hurried return to Barcelona where a watchful eye can be kept on Alejandro and Juan Enrique.

Sometimes the overseas trips can involve quite short journeys and provide a relaxing sojourn. It was, for example, only a few hours drive northwards to help Moura Lympany establish a Music Festival in 1981 in her holiday home village of Rasiguères, near Perpignan in the Pyrenees. And the week-long summer festival of music making was pure un-trammelled enjoyment for Victoria. Sometimes the near inac-cessibility of a festival, like the one held in Italy in Torre del Lago, calls for a combination of plane, train and car as gruelling as any faced by Victoria and her mother when they slept on one another's shoulders on the wooden compartment seats when it all started in the 1940s. On such occasions, the contact with the public is the great reward that ensures a contented return to Spain before the next series of tours.

In between them Victoria alternates preparations for the next concert with running her home. It is a good time to see members of her family and to meet her sister for shopping expeditions in Barcelona. On these occasions relatives report that she frequently indulges in acts of impulsive generosity which used to startle them but which they accept now as a part of her nature. If a disabled child is encountered in a store he is likely to be whisked off on an impromptu shop-ping expedition. If a group of hungry open-handed gypsy children are encountered in the street, they are loaded with meat and fruit hastily gathered together on a whirlwind spree of nearby shops.

Family bonds are occasionally renewed in Victoria's professional life as well when she gives one of her rare recitals on home ground. These never take place in Barce-lona itself. The setting of an ancient cathedral or venerable Catalan church or monastery a few hours' drive outside the city is always chosen. In such historic places, those who really wish to hear the voice of the artist who grew up in their home city in the 1940s can still do so. On these occasions Victoria's sister, Carmen, is usually present as unofficial dresser cum confidante as she often used to be in the old days. And, sometimes, one of Pepe's sons comes along to turn over the sheets of music for his aunt's accompanist. These concerts—like the one given in the Cathedral-like church of Castellón de Ampurias on a recent Palm Sunday— tend to be big occasions, with Victoria and her audience sometimes near to tears. Is it perhaps the last time they will hear her sing?

'I may stop singing for any one of several reasons. Maybe I just will not want to sing any more. Perhaps I shall not be able to because of my children. But I shall never announce that I am retiring. One day I shall just not be there any more.'

Discography

For almost all of her recording career, Victoria de los Angeles has been under exclusive contract to EMI (HMV). The following recordings have therefore been released on the HMV/ ANGEL (USA) labels. They are listed in chronological order of UK release dates.

Recordings on 78s

Composer	Title	Reference No	UK Release Date
Falla	La vida breve 'Vivan los que rien' and 'Alli esta Riyendo'	DB 6702	June 1948
Granados	'El Mirar de la Maja'	DA 1913	July 1949
Fuste	'Hablame de Amores'		
Gounod	Faust 'Il était un roi de Thule' and 'O Dieu! que de bijoux!'	DB 6938	October 1949
Turina	Farruca	DA 1926	December 1949
Valverde	Clavelitos		
Respighi	Stornellatrice E se un giorno tornasse	DA 1930	February 1950

Composer	Title	Reference No	UK Release Date
Massenet	*Manon* 'Adieu notre petite table'	DB 6994	March 1950
Mozart	*Le Nozze di Figaro.* Porgi Amor		
Turina	Saeta Cantares	DA 1929	May 1950
Wagner	*Tannhäuser* 'Dich teure Halle'	DB 21095	September 1950
	Lohengrin 'Einsam in truben Tagen'		
Granados	La Maja y el ruiseñor (Sung with orchestra; conducted Fistoulari)	DB 21069	November 1950
Guridi	No quiero tus avellanas Jota	DA 1961	January 1951
Granados	La Maja Dolorosa No 3 El Majo Discreto	DA 1976	May 1951
Traditional	Spanish songs with Renata Tarrago (guitar)	DA 1970/75	September 1951
Traditional	Spanish Songs with Renata and Graciano Tarrago	DA 1977	July 1952
Falla	Seven popular Spanish Songs	DB 9731/2	February 1952
Brahms Schumann	Von ewiger Liebe Der Nussbaum Accompanied Gerald Moore	DB 21457	May 1952
Rossini	*Il barbiere di Siviglia* 'una voce poco fa'	DA 2030	March 1953
Rossini	'All 'idea di quel metallo' 'Se il mio nome'	DB 21576	June 1953
Nin arranged	El vito Pano murciano	DA 2046	September 1953
Vives	El retrato de Isabela El amor y los ojos	DA 2059	April 1954

Composer	Title	Reference No	UK Release Date

Complete Opera (and Highlights)

Composer	Title	Reference No	UK Release Date
Rossini	*The Barber of Seville* Milan Symphony Orchestra conducted by Serafin with Becchi, Monti and Rossi-Lemeni)	ALP 1022/4	December 1952
Leoncavallo	*I Pagliacci* (RCA Victor Orchestra conducted by Cellini with Björling and Warren)	ALP 1126/7 Import Seraphim	April 1954
Puccini	*Suor Angelica* (Rome Opera Orchestra conducted by Serafin)	ALP 1577	May 1954
Falla	*La vida breve* (Barcelona Opera Orchestra conducted by Halffter with Gomez, Civil.) Song Recital of Spanish Songs with Gerald Moore.	ALP 1150/1	July 1954
Gounod	*Faust* (Paris Opera Orchestra conducted by Cluytens with Christoff and Gedda)	ALP 1162/5	September 1954
Puccini	*Madama Butterfly* (Rome Opera Orchestra and Chorus. Conducted by Cavazzeni with di Stefano and Gobbi)	ALP 1215/7	February 1955
Massenet	*Manon* (Opéra Comique Orchestra conducted by Monteux with Legay)	ALP 1394/7 SLS 5119	November 1956
Puccini	*La Bohème* (RCA Victor Orchestra and Chorus conducted by Beecham. With Björling, Merrill, Tozzi and Amara)	ALP 1409/10 SLS 896	December 1956
Debussy	*Pelléas et Mélisande* (RDF Orchestra conducted by Cluytens with Jensen and Souzay)	ALP 1522/4	November 1957

171

Composer	Title	Reference No	UK Release Date
Verdi	*Simon Boccanegra* (Rome Opera Orchestra conducted by Santini with Gobbi, Christoff and Campora)	ALP 1634/6 SLS 5090	November 1958
Puccini	*Gianni Schicchi* (Rome Opera Orchestra conducted by Santini with Gobbi)	ALP 1726 m ASD 295 s	September 1959
Gounod	*Faust* (Paris Opera and Chorus conducted by Cluytens with Christoff and Gedda)	ALP 1721/4 m ASD 307/10 s SLS 816	November 1959
Bizet	*Carmen* (RDF Orchestra conducted by Beecham with Gedda)	ALP 1762/4 m ASD 331/3 s SLS 5021	February 1960
Verdi	*La Traviata* (Rome Opera Orchestra and Chorus conducted by Serafin with Del Monte and Sereni)	ALP 1780/2 m ASD 359/61 s SLS 5097	September 1960
Puccini	*Madama Butterfly* (Rome Opera Orchestra and Chorus conducted by Santini with Björling)	ALP 1795/7 m ASD 373/5 s SLS 5128	November 1960
Gounod	*Faust* Highlights Re-issue	ALP 1837 m ASD 412 s	August 1961
	The Beecham Recordings. Re-issue	ALP 1870/1	December 1961
Verdi	*La Traviata* Highlights Re-issue	S 35822	November 1961 (Issued in USA not UK)
Puccini	*La Bohème* Highlights Re-issue.	ALP 1921 ESD 7023	December 1962
Mascagni	*Cavalleria rusticana* (Rome Opera orchestra conducted by Santini with Corelli)	AN 108/9 m SAN 108/95/63 s	May 1963

Composer	Title	Reference No	UK Release Date
Rossini	*Il barbiere di Siviglia* (RPO with Glyndebourne Festival Chorus conducted by Gui with Alva and Bruscantini)	AN 114/6 m SAN 114/6 s SLS 5165	October 1963
Bizet	*Carmen* Highlights Re-issue	ALP 2041 m ASD 590 s ESD 7047	September 1964
Puccini	*Madama Butterfly* Highlights Re-issue	ALP 2060 m ASD 609 s	November 1964
Verdi	*Simon Boccanegra* Highlights Re-issue	ALP 2067	February 1965
Offenbach	*The Tales of Hoffmann* (Paris Conservatoire Orchestra conducted by Cluytens with Gedda, D'Angelo and Schwarzkopf)	AN 154/6 m SAN 154/6 s	November 1965
Massenet	*Manon* Highlights Re-issue	ALP 2105	November 1965
Various	Gerald Moore: The Supreme Accompanist	HQM 1072	
Falla	*La vida breve* (Spanish National Orchestra conducted by Frühbeck de Burgos with Cossutta. Coupled with Granados Tonadillas accompanied by Soriano)	AN 157/8 m SAN 157/8 s	March 1966
	Arias from Operas Re-issue	ASD 2274	August 1966
Purcell	*Dido and Aeneas* (English Chamber Orchestra conducted by Barbirolli with Glossop)	SAN 169 SXLP 30275	October 1966
Rossini	*Il barbiere di Siviglia* Highlights	X ASD 2307	April 1967
Offenbach	*Tales of Hoffmann* Highlights	X ASD 2330	November 1967

173

Composer	Title	Reference No	UK Release Date
Massenet	*Werther* (Orchestre de Paris conducted by Prêtre with Gedda, Mesplé, Benoit)	SAN 249/51 SLS 5105	February 1970

Other LP Recordings

Composer	Title	Reference No	UK Release Date
Traditional	Seventeen Traditional Spanish Songs (Accompanied Renata Tarrago—guitar)	ALP 1063	December 1953
Falla	Seven Popular Spanish Songs	BLP 1037	February 1954
Berlioz Debussy	Nuits d'été La Damoiselle élue (Boston Symphony Orchestra, conducted Munch)	ALP 1368	September 1956
	Five Centuries of Spanish Song	ALP 1393	October 1956
Turina	Canta a Sevilla London Symphony Orchestra Cond. Fistoulari	ALP 1185	November 1954
	Italian Arias (Rome Opera Orchestra conducted by Morelli) 'L'altra Notte' (Boito's *Mefistofele*), 'Ebben Ne andro lontana' (Catalani's *La Wally*), 'Voi lo sapete' (Mascagni's *Cavalleria*), 'Me chiamano Mimì' and 'Donde lieta usci' (Puccini's *Bohème*), 'Nacqui all' affano' and 'Non piu mesta' (Rossini's *Cenerentola*), 'Ernani involami' (Verdi's *Ernani*), 'Era piu calmo' (Verdi's *Otello*), 'Piangea cantando', 'Ave Maria'	ALP 1284	November 1956
	Highlights from *I Pagliacci*	ALP 1481	September 1957

Composer	Title	Reference No	UK Release Date
Villa-Lobos	Bachianas Brasileiras Nos 2, 5, 6, 9 RDF orchestra conducted by Villa-Lobos	ALP 1603 ALP 3803	September 1959
	The Fabulous Victoria de los Angeles	ALP 1838 ASD 413	August 1961
	Spanish Songs of the Renaissance with the *Ars Musicae* Ensemble of Barcelona	ALP 1883 m ASD 452 s	March 1962
	Duets with Fischer-Dieskau Accompanied by Gerald Moore	ALP 1891 ASD 459	April 1962
Falla Granados	Popular Songs Tonadillas	ALP 1911 m ASD 479 s	September 1962
Montsalvatge Rodrigo Falla	Cinco canciones negras Quatro madrigales amatorios Vivanlos que rien	ALP 1954 m ASD 505 s	December 1962
Fauré	*Requiem* (Paris Conservatoire Orchestra conducted by Cluytens with Fischer-Dieskau)	AN 107 m SAN 107 s CFP 40234	June 1963
Ravel	Schéhérazade Deux Mélodies hébraïques Cinq Mélodies populaires grecques	ALP 1979 m ASD 530 s	May 1963
Duparc	*Invitation au voyage Phidylé* (Paris Conservatoire Orch.—Prêtre)		
	Great Sopranos of Our Time	ALP 2008 m ASD 558 s	December 1963
Falla	El sombrero de tres picos (Philharmonia Orchestra conducted by Frühbeck de Burgos)	ALP 2059 m ASD 608 s SXLP 30187	November 1964
	A World of Song (LSO conducted by Frühbeck de Burgos)	ALP 2104 m ASD 651 s	October 1965

Composer	Title	Reference No	UK Release Date
Ravel Debussy Ravel	Schéhérazade L'Année en vain Cinq Mélodies populaires grecques Spanish Songs	ASD 2260	April 1966
Debussy	Fêtes galantes (First Series) Noël des enfants qui n'ont plus de maison Trois chansons de Bilitis	ASD 2287	April 1967
Fauré	Roses d'Ispahan Toujours Tristesse		
Hahn	Rossignol des lilas Trois jours de vendages		
Ravel	Chants populaires		
	Homage to Gerald Moore with Fischer-Dieskau and Schwarzkopf	SAN 182/3 SLS 926	May 1967
	History of Music in Sound – Vol. 5	HLP 11	
	Grand Gala of Operatic Ensembles	ASD 2324	August 1967
Berlioz	L'Enfance du Christ (Paris Conservatoire Orchestra conducted by Cluytens with Gedda)	SAN 170/1	October 1967
	Gala of Opera Duets	ASD 2382	July 1968
	Songs of Andalucia Vol 1. (Ars Musicae Ensemble conducted by Gispert)	SAN 194	August 1968
	Songs From Zarzuelas cond. Frühbeck de Burgos	ASD 2415	February 1969
	Gerald Moore Seventieth Birthday	SAN 255	June 1969
	Songs of Catalonia	ASD 2517	February 1970
	Spanish Popular Songs (Accompanied Zanetti)	ASD 2649	January 1972

176

Composer	Title	Reference No	UK Release Date
Falla	El amor brujo (conducted by Giulini)	CX 5265 SAX 5265 SXLP 30140	
	Song Recital including Schubert, Brahms	SXLP 30147	July 1972
Chausson	Poème de l'amour	ASD 2826	March 1973
Canteloube	Chants d'Auvergne		
	Hunter College Recital with Alicia de Larrocha	USA S 36896	Not issued in UK
	The Incomparable Victoria de los Angeles Three Record Set Spanish Songs and arias from *Faust, Tannhäuser, Lohengrin, Il barbiere di Siviglia, Madama Butterfly, Cavalleria rusticana, Otello, Manon, La Bohème, Carmen, La vida breve*	SLS 5012	July 1975
	More Songs of the Auvergne	ASD 3134	November 1975
	In concert at the Festival Hall	ASD 3656	July 1979
Vivaldi	*Orlando Furioso* Role of Angelica with I Solisti Veneti Conducted by Scimone	Erato STU 71138	1977
Recital	Moreno 4 Aztec Songs Bautista 3 Songs dedicated to Andalusian Cities	CBS 76833	1978
	Albeniz 6 Songs to Italian Texts Rodrigo 4 Sephardic Songs Accompanist Geoffrey Parsons		
	In preparation: The Art of Victoria de los Angeles	SLS 5233	
	Arias by Handel and Mozart	ASD 4193	

Acknowledgments

The illustrations are reproduced by kind permission of the following:

Illustrations between pages 56 and 57—(page 1) top left & right, bottom left, *José Maria Lamaña*; (page 2) bottom right, *José Maria Lamaña*; (page 3) *José Maria Lamaña*; (page 5) top, *Mateo-Fotos, Barcelona*, bottom, *Suárez, Barcelona*; (page 6) top, *John Heddon, London*, bottom, *José Maria Lamaña*; (page 7) *EMI Records Ltd (UK)*; (page 8) top, *Metropolitan Opera, New York*, bottom, *Alan Sievewright*.

Illustrations between pages 88 and 89—(page .1) top, *EMI Records Ltd (UK)*, bottom, *Metropolitan Opera, New York (photo: Sedge Le Blang)*; (page 2) top, *E. Piccagliani, Teatro alla Scala, Milan*, bottom, *Publifoto, Milan*; (page 3) *E. Piccagliani, Teatro alla Scala, Milan*; (page 4) top, *Metropolitan Opera, New York*, bottom left, *Metropolitan Opera, New York (photo: Sedge Le Blang)*, bottom right, *Metropolitan Opera, New York*; (page 5) *Metropolitan Opera, New York*; (page 6) top, *Alan Sievewright*, bottom, *Anthony Crickmay, London*; (page 7) top, *Metropolitan Opera, New York*, bottom, *EMI Records Ltd (UK) (photo: Rudolph Betz)*.

Illustrations between pages 120 and 121—(page 1) bottom, *Wayne J. Shilkret, New York*; (page 2) *Louis Mélançon, New York*; (page 3) top, *Metropolitan Opera, New York*, bottom, *Particam Pictures, Amsterdam (photo: Henk Jonker)*; (page 5) bottom, *Fotos RAS, Barcelona*; (page 6) top, *Eleanor Morrison*, bottom, *EMI Records Ltd (UK)*; (page 7) bottom, *Torres Molina-Foto, Granada*; (page 8) left, *A. Saenz-Guerrero, Barcelona*.

Illustrations between pages 152 and 153—(page 1) top, *EMI Records Ltd (UK)*, bottom, *Electrola Gessellschaft mbH, Köln-Braunsfeld*; (page 2) top, *EMI Records Ltd (UK)*, bottom, *EMI Records Ltd (UK) (photo: Axel Poignant)*; (page 3) *Segui Fotografo, Barcelona*; (page 4) *BBC Copyright, British Broadcasting Corporation, London*; (page 5) top, left & right, *Nigel Luckhurst, Cambridge*; (page 6) *EMI Records Ltd (UK) (photo: Segui, Barcelona)*; (page 7) *José Maria Lamaña (EMI Records)*; (page 8) *Clive Barda, London*.

Index

179

181